The Wedding of

and

at

on

jacqui
small

How to Plan your Wedding

Contents

Introduction

Congratulations on your engagement! It is 26 years since I went down the aisle with my soulmate for my own perfect country wedding. My husband Peter and I were married in the church where my parents had wed 37 years earlier, and had a marquee festooned with flowers in the garden of my parents' home in Suffolk. Back then most of the information about how to plan a wedding came from etiquette books, and there were still some very strong traditions concerning weddings.

Since then, the wedding industry has exploded into a multimillion-pound industry and the choices are immense and daunting for each bride and groom. The global scale of the wedding business is also a factor in how long it now takes to plan a wedding. Most wedding dresses are made in China in factories owned by the major bridal designers. You may think you have picked a gown from a famous Spanish bridal house but the chances are that your made-to-measure gown will be shipped in from China. Most bridal houses require you to choose your dress up to six months ahead of time so you can manage two fittings before your big day. Popular venues also get booked up a year or more in advance.

For the last 25 years I have worked on thousands of weddings on all different scales, budgets and all over the world. As the choices have widened and weddings have become more unique or complicated, I have witnessed at firsthand how daunting it is to plan your own wedding. I have worked with countless clients over a year to six months from our first introduction to the 'production' of their wedding day. I have had the pleasure of working with some of the best wedding planners, event coordinators, top caterers, and in a huge range of venues, so I have come to understand and know the wedding industry inside out and how to plan the perfect wedding.

This book includes all the advice you need to plan a sublime wedding day. I know it works because I have helped numerous love-struck couples who have had the 'best day of their lives'. Read the advice from some of the UK's best wedding suppliers and use this book to plan an effortless and accomplished wedding.

Enjoy planning your gig day and embarking on the next exciting chapter of your life with your perfect partner!

OPPOSITE A table centre made up of white peonies, with 'Margaret Merril', 'Julia's Baby' and 'Vendela' roses, cream double eustoma, white sweet pea, *Alchemilla mollis*, variegated weigela and *Eucalyptus parvifolia*.

Paula's top ten tips

1 Don't get stressed. Remember, planning is the key. Use this planner to keep you on track and stick to the dates and the timeline. Keep calm and keep carefully ticking 'to-do' things off your list each week in the countdown to the wedding.

2 Share the important decisions with your fiancé and choose between you which tasks are best suited to your talents and abilities. Delegate every task you can. If you are not the most organized person in the world, align yourself with a friend to help who has great organizational skills. Play to people's strengths; look around your friends for their talents and use their unique skills, from baking cakes to calligraphy.

3 Choose suppliers you connect with. Some of them are going to share your special day with you. Make sure you know and like your photographer as he or she is going to be on your coat tails all day, from getting ready to going away.

4 Dress rehearsals put everyone at ease, and it is always a good idea to get your major players together ahead of time so they can work as a team. They are not just there to be decorative, so make sure they know what is expected of them on the day. Consider a rehearsal dinner the night before or the penultimate evening.

5 Don't put too much pressure on yourself to lose weight or have a great tan. Be wary of spray tans and radical changes of style on the day. Practise hair and make-up so you know you are going to feel confident and on top form. Waterproof mascara, long-lasting lipstick, water and tissues are a must for the big day.

6 Have a fun evening the night before, but make sure you get to bed early. Try to get a good eight hours' sleep so you look your best, and have a healthy protein breakfast. Arrange hair and make-up appointments early so that you can spend the last few hours of your single life with your family or close friends.

7 If things don't go to plan, don't let it ruin your special day. Usually only the bride knows what has not gone to plan and the other guests won't notice if you keep quiet and smile through. Go with the flow and don't worry about anything. Have a plan for whatever the weather may do, rain or shine. The weather is often the big unknown, so keep calm and cheerful whatever the forecast.

OPPOSITE A ring of 'Milano' and 'Colandro' roses, 'Kansas' peonies, 'Tango' leucospermums, 'Lill Orange' zinnias, *Achillea* 'Moonshine', *Viburnum opulus* berries and *Corylus maxima* 'Red Filbert'.

8 Have a first-kiss moment at the appropriate time and remember it is about your day as a couple. It sounds strange, but too many couples forget to enjoy their wedding day. Try to stay together so you experience the day as a couple.

9 Don't run away on honeymoon too soon. It can be a very emotional time just after your wedding and so a brunch with close friends and family the next day is a lovely way of extending the event in a relaxed mood.

10 Radiate happiness – it is infectious. The best weddings are the ones when the bride and groom are hopelessly in love and their happiness is contagious. All you need is love for a perfect wedding on any scale, budget or location.

Your Big Day

how to begin to plan
your wedding

One of the greatest privileges of being a floral designer has been working with so many brides and grooms on planning their big day. So many couples have been so grateful for the help and advice that they have received that they have suggested I put it all down in this book to help other couples plan their perfect day.

Unless you a natural organizer and list maker, planning your own wedding is an incredible accomplishment. You are new to the business, so it is hard even to make a start. There are simply so many things to think about, decide on and then activate from the date, time, venue, to the wording on the invitations and even who to invite. Then you have to persuade, negotiate, hunt, prioritize, appease, source, order, pursue and sometimes placate and compromise all at the same time. Then comes the bartering, more negotiating or trimming and the finalizing. No wonder the term 'Bridezilla' has appeared all over the media – there is so much to consider and make a decision on! Finally, there are all the collections and deliveries to coordinate, and making sure that it all goes to plan on the day, not to mention keeping to the budget. And you've got to achieve all this while probably working full time. The average bride spends the equivalent of six whole weeks on her wedding.

This book is designed to help you plan your wedding and guide you through all the stages with helpful advice from some of the very best wedding professionals that I have had the pleasure to work with. My intention is to help you plan your budget at the beginning, be realistic about what is important to you and then guide you through all the important decisions you have to make. Remember that it is a celebration of the start of your new life together and all your friends and family will be there to support you on this special day. After the excitement of the engagement, it is now important to sit down with your partner and decide together how you want this special day to feel, and what reflects your own personal style, both individually and as a couple. More importantly, this book is to help you enjoy the process of planning a wedding and to assist you in having 'the best day of your life – so far!'

OPPOSITE A striking bridal bouquet of white peonies edged with hosta leaves.

hiring a professional
wedding planner

If you do not have the time to project manage the event, because you are arranging the event in a hurry or are busy with other commitments, it may be worth employing a wedding planner.

As expensive as this might seem at first glance, I am certain that in many ways a planner can save you money as well as time, because they will know how to make the most of your budget. From my experience many couples spend too much time getting multiple quotes from lots of venues, vendors and suppliers, and sometimes become totally confused by the myriad decisions. If you feel that you are agonizing over decisions and procrastinating, you might need to consider having a planner to guide and reassure you. He or she can also take the pressure out of the day itself, so you can really enjoy the event and relax. Just make sure that you feel totally comfortable with your planner and really want to have him or her share the day with you.

'If you have not employed a wedding planner, there will be times when you wonder why you're doing this; it can be stressful at times. When the bills are flying in and you are worrying about all sorts of increasingly inconsequential details, remember that it is all worth it in the end and you will remember your wedding day forever.

Julia Dowling, Snapdragon Parties

'A good wedding planner will be able to interpret your ideas and create a day that has your identity firmly stamped on it. While there is a planning process to follow, a good wedding planner should not work to a template, but create something new each time, taking inspiration from the two of you. This keeps it fresh for us too! Working with a wedding planner will inspire you with new ideas as well as you having the reassurance of knowing that you have someone advising you on what will or will not work each step of the way. Planning your wedding should be a fun experience and not something you feel is another thing to try and fit into your already busy days or weeks; a wedding planner can alleviate this stress and ensure you relish this enjoyable process.'

Siobhan Craven-Robins, wedding coordinator

OPPOSITE Grapes have been wired into these arrangements of 'Con Amore', 'Cool Water', 'Blue Pacific' and 'Christian' roses, with foliage of *Heuchera* 'Plum Pudding' and *Cotinus coggygria* 'Royal Purple'.

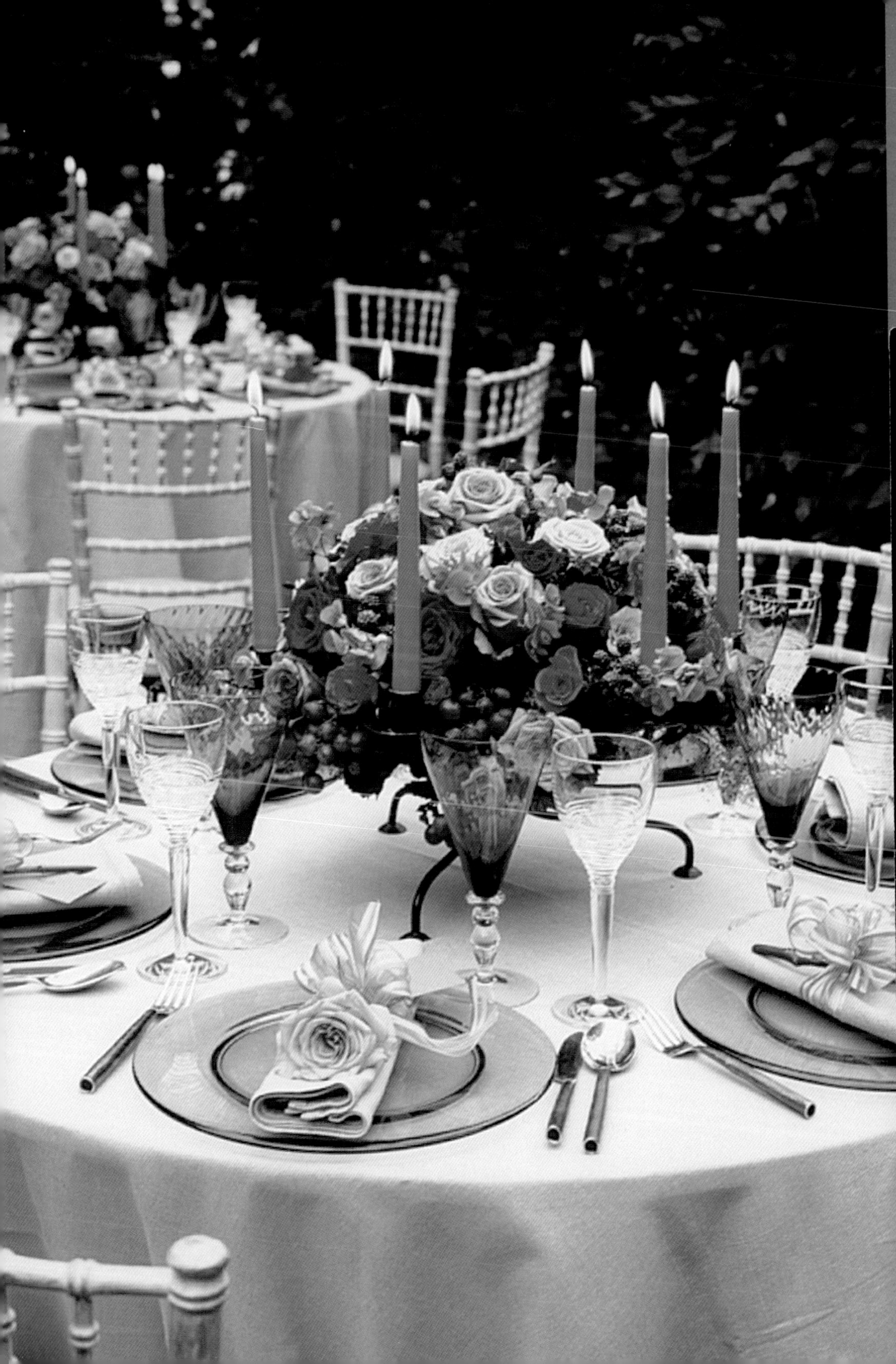

picking your
wedding date

When is the best time to get married? Most brides have a favourite season of the year and this is often the time they want to plan their weddings. If you have a favourite flower that you want to include, then it is always a good idea to check when it is going to be in its prime. With the worldwide distribution of flowers, I have sourced out-of-season flowers from the other side of the world, but this always adds to the costs.

● Spring weddings have a lush palette of flowers to choose from, and this is a must if you want blossom.

● Summer is, of course, the most popular season for weddings and it is lovely if you can have part of your day outside in a garden.

● Autumn weddings can have the backdrop of all the colours of fall, and this is a great season to work some fruits or vegetables into your styling.

● Winter is perfect for a cosy wedding indoors or creating a bit of sparkle with a winter wonderland.

THIS PAGE Shot glasses are filled with snowdrops and sprigs of jasmine, twisted with wire.
OPPOSITE CLOCKWISE FROM TOP LEFT The white daisy Chrysanthemum 'Reagan White'. A basket of 'Gracia' and 'Mimi Eden' spray roses, Alchemilla mollis, Brachyglottis 'Sunshine' and feverfew. A napkin decoration of Helleborus orientalis, ivy and Viburnum tinus. A zinc basket of roses, sweet peas, Astrantia and Brachyglottis 'Sunshine'.

Which day of the week?

This is an important consideration, depending on whether you are having a religious or civil ceremony. The Jewish and Christian Sabbaths mean that Saturday and Sunday are out respectively, and civil register offices are often only open part of the weekend, if at all – usually Saturday mornings. If your budget is tight then planning a wedding on a weekday and not in a popular month might halve some of your costs.

Extra-special occasion

Some couples choose a special day like Valentine's Day or plan a winter wedding near Christmas. Both these times are particularly difficult for flowers and will certainly add to the venue costs.

Caterers are also very busy around Christmas and personally I would advise against the few days between Christmas and New Year when staffing is an issue for all.

Deciding the date

Which season and date would suit you? Are there any particular times you need to avoid? Make a note of work or family commitments, or weddings of friends. Then narrow down your choices.

Confirmed date: ....

OPPOSITE White tulips, *Phalaenopsis* orchids, ranunculus, and lilac have been used in low and tall frosted glasses. Planted snowdrops and miniature succulents in silver cubes mark each place, with pink *Phalaenopsis* orchids on the cake and napkins.

THIS PAGE A bunch of 'Honeymoon' tulips hand-tied and placed in a frosted vase.

selecting a
style and theme

Setting the tone and style for the day should be a joint decision between the bride and groom. Some weddings are rooted in tradition, and vintage and retro are also current trends. Other couples want to have very original and unusual weddings and go out of their way to avoid anything conventional. For some, the venue or the location will invite a theme, whether urban, country, fairytale, modern – it can be whatever your heart desires.

Colour is one of the easiest tools with which to create a theme and give your event continuity. This is most often reflected in the colour of the attendants' outfits and also the flower colour. White and green or white and ivory continue to be the most popular colour choices. Consistency in your style and theme will create a more coordinated look. Sometimes I think that brides can take this to the extreme, and when one begins to tell me the nail polish colour of the mother of the bride, I realize it has taken on obsessional proportions!

Home-made personal touches make any celebration unique. Ask talented friends to help you make the event more special, but don't put too much pressure on yourself or them, as you need to be as relaxed as possible to create a really good celebration.

Many couples get carried away with the budget in planning the wedding, so it is always a good idea to agree the look and feel of the wedding together, and revisit this idea if the budget starts to spiral out of control.

OPPOSITE A white theme incorporates gypsophila, 'Vendela' roses, massed hydrangea, peonies and sweet peas with polished shells and ivory table linen.
THIS PAGE Herbs and garden flowers such as blossom and hellebores create a natural feel.

Mackenzie Grant

putting together a
DIY wedding

Delegation and organization are key to the do-it-yourself wedding. Many couples choose this route because they want their event to be more personal and individual. I think you need to be realistic about numbers and timing if you are going to attempt to do a lot of the work yourself.

THIS PAGE Decorative glass jars are filled with sweet peas and suspended by wires.
OPPOSITE Group different garden flowers in glass bottles tied together with raffia. Individual rose-petal Bundt cakes on vintage plates are an alternative to a full-scale wedding cake.

● Keep catering costs down by having canapés, bowl food or a buffet. Barbecue or hog roast caterers are also less expensive options, and remember, if you don't have a formal meal, you need less in the way of equipment and hire.

● Be savvy about the time of year and day of the week that you choose to marry and you can cut the costs to a minimum.

● Limit your guest numbers to fewer than 100. Most people who have been married will tell you that their wedding was the last time they saw certain friends and family. Any marriage marks a new chapter in your life and your patterns of friendship naturally change. If children come along later, you inevitably have less time for your old friends and make new ones through your children and their play friends. My advice would be to always think about having a smaller wedding rather than stretch a small budget too far. Some of the best weddings I have seen have been perfectly formed for about 20 really close friends and family.

An eco wedding

A 'green' wedding may be your aim, and this is certainly a new and popular trend. There are websites devoted to this idea and also some wedding fairs. Some venues offer this kind of event too. Buffets of simple, fresh, organic fare are often served with local home-grown wines. Use plants that can be recycled in your home or garden or given to guests. Keep the numbers manageable and hire a simple marquee for your garden or a local hall.

THIS PAGE A glass bowl is lined with leaves and floral foam and filled with ivy berries, eustoma, hydgrangea and 'Talea', 'Sweet Akito' and 'Espérance' roses.
OPPOSITE Hydrangea and roses grouped around an elegant candelabra, with rose petals decorating the base of the candles.

making it
stylish and impressive

The decoration and style of a wedding is what separates one from another and makes it memorable to all its guests. A truly stylish wedding makes a lasting impression through all the little details. Usually this is a joint effort between your floral designer and your caterer, who will work together to create the ambiance you desire.

Any professional wedding florist will be able to elevate your event by suggesting items to rent from local companies and also from their own warehouses, where they have a diversity of treasure to enhance any event. From this plethora of props your event can be personalized and made unique, from huge urns and plinths for dramatic flower displays, or giant candelabras for the tables, down to small posies tied with organza ribbon onto the napkins.

Beautiful linens are one of my priorities, and there are also lots of wonderful hire companies online from whom you can rent just the right cut-glass flute or perfect charger plate. Your caterer will offer you a huge range of rentals to choose

THIS PAGE Autumnal table arrangement with hydrangea, purple lisianthus, gloriosa, snowberries, ivy berries, 'Milano' roses and guelder roses.

OPPOSITE A large classical arrangement in an urn features 'Concordia' lilies, forsythia, foxgloves, hydrangea, peonies, chrysanthemums, fountain grass and hypericum.

from for your table, and you can see these all come together at a tasting. Often this will also be the time when your florist will display their ideas for the table.

Increasingly, venues also offer wedding stylists who work alongside florists with fabric and other artefacts, such as huge chandeliers and giant mirrors, to decorate your venue. Furniture rental companies offer you a vast choice, from modern and zen to the baroque and luxurious. The choice of chairs or chair covers can transform a room or setting.

Lighting is also a very important component of your decoration and your floral designer will help advise you on which companies to use and what kind of effects work best with their floral designs. When it comes to decorative details, the possibilities are truly endless.

setting your
budget

There is no doubt that weddings have become more lavish and complex over the last quarter of a century. Even if you are planning a grand and sumptuous wedding, it is always wise to set a maximum budget. Some couples and families add up a list of costs from their 'want list' and work backwards or upwards, and this is often a recipe for financial ruin. Everyone has different ideas on what is important and how they want to spend their money, and it can also lead to tensions and family arguments. Don't run out and order or buy anything until you have agreed on the bottom line.

Having a budget breakdown also focuses your efforts – you won't waste time looking at services and acquiring quotes for more than you can afford. All suppliers and vendors are more able to help you achieve your goal if they know what it is you have in your budget. I much prefer to work with clients who tell me their outline budget and ask me how to make the most impact for that price.

The largest ticket item is going to be the catering and the drink, and so you need to decide early on what kind of reception you can afford. A seated dinner for 400 is going to be a lot more expensive than an afternoon tea reception for 100 guests. Start by contacting recommended caterers and get a feel for the kind of costs involved for your perfect reception. Also check out the costs of the venue or marquee hire, and you will begin to outline your largest costs, which could be as much as 50 per cent of the overall bill.

Another important thing to consider is the taxation due on certain items. For example, in the UK 20 per cent VAT (value added tax) is often added on top of quotes, which makes a huge difference to initial costings. Also ask your suppliers or vendors about what gratuities might be expected. Remember, too, that if your event runs later or goes over the agreed schedule time, you will also incur added costs, as the overtime rate spirals. All venues need to have their spaces cleared for re-hire the next day, and there will be a team ready and waiting to de-rig and clear your event.

OPPOSITE A candelabra decorated with ruscus, eucalyptus, ivy, *Alchemilla mollis* and garden roses.

Wedding planner rates vary. Usually they are 10–15 per cent of the total event, but some charge as much as 20 per cent for top-of-the-range weddings. You can also find some planners who charge flat fees or will help you out with specific areas for a lesser fee. All wedding planners have different options and scales of charges, and these vary from city to country and also from country to country. There are many independent wedding planners and some bodies that regulate wedding planners.

Insurance

When planning your wedding day you don't want to focus on anything negative or unpleasant. However, it is always advisable to purchase event insurance to provide cover for those unexpected dramas that life throws up occasionally. This should be around 1 per cent for an average wedding, though larger budgets would require a special policy, and if you have important/famous guests the policy creeps up more! As the host of a party with lots of different suppliers and guests, you are in a position of responsibility, and it makes sense to get covered for anything that might go wrong. This gives you peace of mind and makes the run-up to the event less stressful.

Where the money goes...
When you are planning a wedding, this is how
the costs might be proportionately split.

Bridesmaids' outfits
and formal wear

Ceremony

Food and drink

Reception entertainment,
lighting and production

Contingency
and insurance

Stationery

Flowers and
decoration

Transport

Gown and accessories

Cake

Photographer and
videographer

Venue and rentals

Gifts and favours

Accommodation

Hair and make-up

Managing your budget

	Estimate	Deposit	Balance due	Actual
Ceremony				
Marriage licence				
Officiant fee or donation				
Venue hire				
Rings				
Transport				
Other costs				
Choir/bell ringers				
Hire of chuppah				
Reception				
Marquee				
Catering				
Wedding cake				
Bar/mixologist				
Musicians/DJ				
Favours/gifts/gratuities				
Other costs				
Flowers				
Ceremony venue				
Reception venue				
Bride & bridesmaids				
Groom & groomsmen				
Buttonholes & corsages				
Other flowers				
Sub-Total				

	Estimate	Deposit	Balance due	Actual

Attire

Wedding gown

Shoes & accessories

Bridesmaids' outfits

Groom's outfit

Best man's outfit

Groomsmen's outfits

Hairdressing & make-up

Other costs

Photography

Photographer

Videographer

Other costs

Stationery

Invitations

Announcements

Thank-you notes

Other costs

Wedding Insurance

Premium

Other

Various extras

Grand Total

timetable for
perfect planning

Most brides have a year or more to plan, so this is a guideline to what you should consider at each stage. If you have less time, don't panic. Use this list as a prompt and adapt it to your timings. Try to take a few days off work at the outset to secure the venue and your main suppliers, as these are the key decisions. If you have very limited time, consider hiring a wedding planner to help you out and choose a venue that has recommended suppliers or even a restaurant, where there is less to organize.

Date

12 to 18 months before

Work out how many guests you want to invite

Find a venue/venues for the ceremony and reception

Pick a wedding date and time –
check with your venue and important guests
before finalizing

Decide whether to appoint a wedding planner

Decide on the style of your wedding

Draw up a budget

8-10 months before

Shop for your wedding gown

Select your wedding party

Research your wedding professionals

Book your photographer and videographer

Get quotes for catering,
floral decorations and entertainment

Buy a wedding insurance policy

Register your gift list

Choose rings

ABOVE Roses veronica, ranunculus, hyacinths and amaranthus top a glass bowl of coloured mints.

18 months   12 months   6 months   Your wedding day

Date

6-8 months before

Send Save the Date cards

Order outfits for the bridal party

Order the wedding cake

Begin your playlists for your reception

Secure make-up and hair stylists

4-6 months before

Order invitations

Hire a calligrapher

Hire wedding-day transport

Book hotel accommodation

Finalize your menus and flowers

3 months before

Mail invitations

Shop for wedding accessories

Finalize your entertainment and playlist for the DJ

Decide on your vows, music, etc.

Place order for your Order of Service cards

Purchase gifts for your attendants

ABOVE A bouquet of roses, calendula, mini gerberas, celosia and gloriosa.

THIS PAGE A scented bouquet of sweet peas, jasmine, peonies, astrantia and ranunculus.
OPPOSITE Hand-tied domes of sweet william in plain white mugs.

18 months   12 months   6 months   Your wedding day

Date

1 month before

Final fitting of the gown

Give place cards to calligrapher

Finalize all details with suppliers

Have a trial make-up and hair-style session

Give a list of shots to your photographer

Write speeches

Chase any guests who have not replied

2 weeks before

Finish seating plan

Give final seating and numbers to the caterer

Make sure all suppliers have been paid

Make arrangements for outstanding final accounts

Give the plan of the day to the best man
and chief bridesmaid (see pages 40–41)

1 week before

Plan a rehearsal and have dinner with bridal party

Make sure you have collected all outfits

Book in your manicure and pedicure

planning your
schedule of the day

It is essential that you plan the schedule of the day itself. If you are not working with a wedding planner you need to give this task to your best man or best woman, or someone who is prepared to keep a clear head, be calm and keep to the schedule. The timing of the event is essential to its running smoothly, without any glitches, hitches or hold-ups.

A schedule of the day should be drawn up and given to all suppliers so that it is perfectly clear what you are expecting from them, and so they can perform and achieve this for you. There will be many suppliers involved and they will all be independent companies. It is always a good idea to get them all to meet at your wedding venue ahead of time and go through the running of the day. It helps them to all work as a team to fulfil your vision.

If you do not have an event planner, wedding planner or a friend to keep you on track, you need to think about employing a Master of Ceremonies. An MC, as they are known, will often be recommended by your venue and their role is to be the official host of the event and keep it running to time. For the bridal couple and the respective families, this day goes in a furious whirl. I guarantee that when all is done and dusted, a six-hour event will feel like an hour. When you and your new partner have time to reflect, the one thing that you will remember is how the day seemed to fast forward like no other. It will be like watching a time-lapsed film speeded up; you will have no concept of time. Lots of brides choose not to wear a watch and that adds to the 'lost in the moment' feeling.

It is important to keep to the plan because there is so much to distract the bride and groom when they are in a room full of their nearest and dearest. Meanwhile, the venue, the caterers and all your suppliers will have deadlines they need to meet. Overrunning might not just mean that your dinner is over-done; it will also cost you more as staff hours are elongated. After your fairytale is over, your suppliers need to clear the event, and keeping to time is imperative for a successful function that doesn't incur unexpected costs. To give you some idea of how to start planning the timeline of the day, the next two pages offer some guidelines.

OPPOSITE A shower bouquet of scented gardenia and stephanotis.

Tracking the final countdown

	Time	Contact number
Suppliers		
Florists to set up ceremony		
Florists to set up reception		
Lighting company		
Caterers on site		
Cake to arrive		
Band to arrive		
DJ to arrive		
Other		
Other		
Other		
Bride		
Hair		
Make-up		
Other beauty treatments		
Bridal flowers		
Photographer		
Attendants depart for ceremony		
Bride departs for ceremony		

ABOVE Cut limes line a vase of bouvardia, lilac, calla lilies, roses, cymbidium orchids and *Viburnum tinus*.
OPPOSITE Pink and white marshmallows echo the tones of the ranunculus, roses and tulips.

	Time	Contact number

Groom

Meeting point with groomsmen

Buttonhole/corsage delivery

Depart for ceremony

Greet and seat guests

Ceremony

Arrival of groomsmen

Arrival of guests

Best man and groom take position

Arrival of bride

Signing of the register

Reception

Drinks

Receiving line or introductions

Wedding breakfast

Speeches and toasts

Cutting the cake

First dance

Tossing of bouquet and garter

Send-off of bride and groom

Carriages

After-party

Event strike

The Ceremony

finding a
venue

Traditionally, the location for your wedding ceremony was determined by religious affiliation, personal preference or convenience to family and friends. Now, with the licensing of many historic homes for weddings and even the increase in destination weddings, the choice of venue for the ceremony comes down to the personal preferences of the bride and groom.

If you are choosing a religious ceremony and have a place in mind, the key question is the capacity of the venue and whether it is enough to hold your guests. The next key question is whether the building has any regulations on decorations. Often churches ask for the flowers to be donated to the church, so if you had plans to move the flowers on to your reception venue, it is best to make this plain from the outset. The other key question will concern the timing of your wedding, and whether anyone else will be getting married on the same day. This can be complicated if you had planned for a big installation of flowers. Sometimes brides will share the costs of the flowers with each other when getting married on the same day. In my experience, this is less likely to happen these days, because each bride has unique requirements.

Increasingly, it is popular to choose a venue such as a castle or historic house where you can hold both the ceremony and the reception. This often makes for an easier and cosier event than moving your guests from a synagogue, church, chapel or other sacred building to the reception afterwards. However, if you are scouting for a venue, make sure that the venue's staff are happy to accommodate your requests rather than trying to fit your wedding into their venue space. I've worked with both kinds of attitudes, and it really makes a huge difference if you are allowed to make the venue your own on the day. Some museums, art galleries and historic homes have a lot of restrictions and, although they make a fabulous backdrop to your event, you will have to respect their rules. It is important to see the venue when it is set for a ceremony so you can get a feel for what it will be like on your special day before you book.

OPPOSITE, CLOCKWISE FROM TOP LEFT A Jewish chuppah, or wedding canopy, is decorated with floral swags. Hydrangea, lilies and wheat line the arched entry to a church. White and cream flowers suit ornately decorated venues. Freestanding candelabras of hydrangea, lilies and roses mark the pew ends.

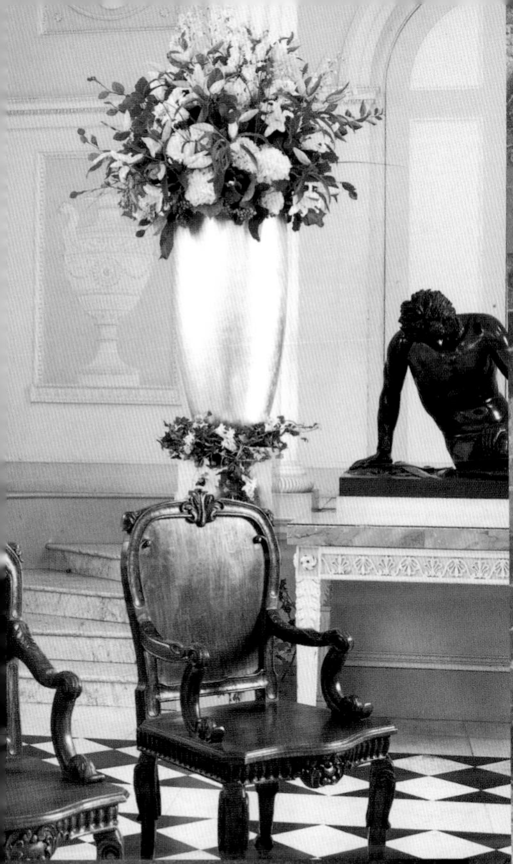

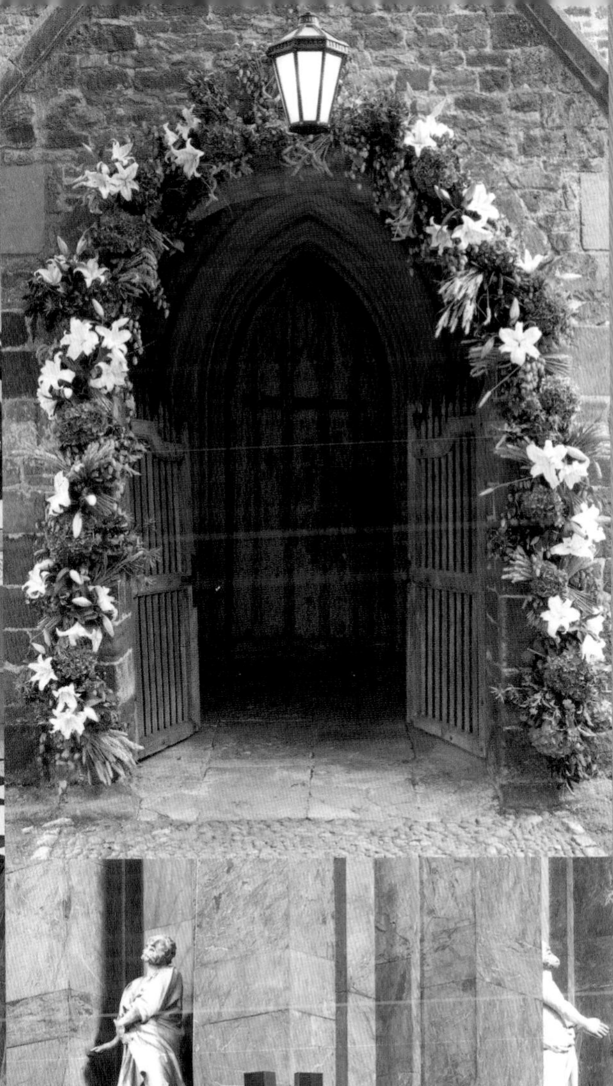

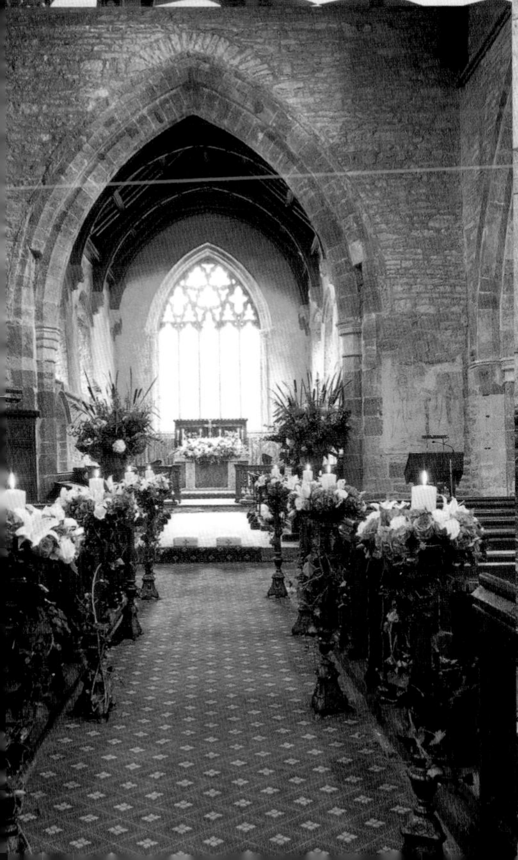

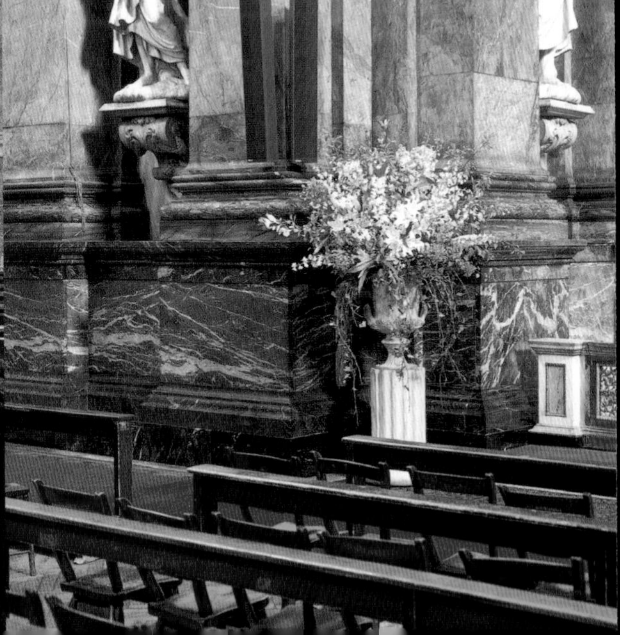

Many hotels offer the chance to have your ceremony and reception in the same place and there are many benefits to holding your wedding on one site. The staff are well trained and used to turning rooms around from the ceremony to the reception. They are also experts at a 'reveal' if you want to surprise your guests with a quick turnaround while they are enjoying their cocktails and canapés. Guests have the option to stay at the hotel, and it avoids complications for travel, disappointing weather and transporting the flowers from ceremony to reception. A hotel can often present less logistical problems than other venues, and allows you to elongate the time you spend with close family and friends, all being in the same place.

Your venue

You will probably visit many venues before you make your final choice. When you have weighed up the pros and cons of each to make your final decision, keep a note here of the details.

Confirmed venue: ....

....

....

....

Contact person: ....

....

Email/telephone: ....

....

Confirmed start and times of ceremony: ....

....

....

....

....

Any restrictions (candles/confetti): ....

....

....

....

OPPOSITE Large freestanding arrangements mark out focal points at a ceremony.

<h1>deciding on your
ceremony flowers</h1>

The floral decorations for your wedding break down into three main areas: bridal-party flowers, ceremony flowers and decorations for the reception. If you are holding your wedding in a religious building you will have to check what is permitted by the caretakers and assistants. Some historic and religious buildings have regulation lists and others are very relaxed. One key element to bear in mind is whether you have the only event on that day or whether other floral decorators may be involved.

For the ceremony, an important area to decorate is the altar area, where usually two large arrangements are placed symmetrically to frame the bridal couple. Floral pew ends also frame the entrance and the processional, and so they are one of my favourite areas to decorate. Freestanding candelabras also work well in larger churches, decorated with flowers and greenery. Many churches have altar vases that can be decorated, but each incumbent will have their own views on how the altar should be decorated as it is one of the most sacred areas of the church. The entrance and the font in conventional churches are other areas to decorate if your budget allows. The officiant/celebrant or register-signing table is also another area to place a low arrangement of flowers. Jewish weddings require decorations under the chuppah, or canopy. Sometimes this is constructed for the occasion, and this allows for some amazing constructions of flowers. If a traditional or family canopy is being used, normally the four columns will be decorated. The bema and the ark are other areas to consider decorating, and often the women's gallery allows for garlands and hanging decorations. Hindu weddings involve the exchange of garlands of flowers and take place under a canopy called a mandap.

The worldwide transportation of flowers means that there is always a good selection to choose from. Flower prices do vary from day to day and they are generally more expensive in the winter when supply is restricted. However, there are always seasonal options, and if your budget is tight you need to opt for more seasonal flowers and foliage. Some flowers are only available for a limited period of time, so if you have your heart set on having a particular variety, you need to do some research into its availability. Lily of the valley is a very popular choice for brides. This is in season in early May and though you can procure lily of the valley throughout the year, it will be very expensive out of season. Peonies are also very popular, and although the season is always getting extended, there are times of the year when it is very hard to get them.

OPPOSITE An altar table is laden with autumnal blue hydrangea, lilies and ruscus.
THIS PAGE A mandap, or canopy, at an Indian wedding ceremony is generously decorated with hydrangea, *Phalaenopsis* orchids, roses, gloriosa and shamrock chrysanthemums.

Working with your florist

If you are using a florist, your designer will be able to guide you through the choices. If you are not good with plant names, it is always a good idea to take some tear sheets or a Pinterest board along to your first meeting. Hopefully all your chosen images will have a theme or a similar colour choice, and this will guide your florist. After the first consultation your florist should be able to give you an estimate for the flowers you have chosen. Floral designers increasingly act as stylists for your wedding, adding lots of props and finishing touches.

If you have decided on a budget, it is always useful to be upfront about this so that your florist can work within it. Often I will meet with brides and grooms several times before the overall design is decided. Your florist should meet with you at the venue, and I often take some flowers to dress fittings to decided what will look best with the wedding gown.

Often people have a wishlist for flowers that exceeds their budget. My advice is always to have one really striking arrangement, rather than lots of small ones, which can get lost. If you need to be sensible with the budget, try to use seasonal flowers and give your florist flexibility with the choice. He or she can buy what is best value at market on the day. If you are on a very low budget, consider having plants rather than arrangements. This can be very effective – favourites of mine are *Phalaenopsis* orchids for an urban look, or lavender for a country look.

One thing that I would always consider when planning your wedding flowers is adding some scent. Sweet peas, lily of the valley, stocks, stephanotis, jasmine, gardenia, freesia, hyacinth and tuberosa are all wedding flowers popular for their fragrance. I also adore using herbs in the foliage, such as rosemary, bay, thyme, marjoram, lavender and mint.

LEFT Hydrangea, delphiniums, echinops, 'Casa Blanca' lilies, agapanthus and 'Iceberg' roses.
OPPOSITE Fatsia leaves, agapanthus and roses are used to decorate chairs.

Your choices for your ceremony flowers

First make a note of your favourite flowers –
think which colours you prefer and consider the season: ....

....

....

....

List the florists you would like to approach: ....

....

....

....

List the areas in the ceremony venue you would ideally like to decorate
to give you an idea of what different arrangements you will need: ....

....

....

....

Confirmed florist: ....

Confirmed details: ....

Confirmed ceremony flower choices: ....

....

....

....

....

selecting your
music

Music is vital to your wedding and creates a wonderful
atmosphere. If you are having a religious ceremony, your officiant
will be able to advise you on popular choices.

A choir or a soloist add to a ceremony, and often couples like to hire a string
quartet or a harpist. If you are hiring professional musicians for your wedding
it is important to tell them if you are recording the event. Whether you are
having a civil or a religious ceremony, it is usual to have a piece of music for
the entrance of the bride and for signing the register.

It is always courteous to inform the celebrant or officiant of your choice
of music and readings in advance of the day. Distributing the order of service
keeps everyone informed and helps the day go smoothly.

Your musical choices

Entrance of the bride: ....

....

....

Hymns: ....

....

....

Signing of the register: ....

....

....

Exit of the bride and groom: ....

....

....

OPPOSITE A wrist corsage of scented gardenia. ABOVE Hydgrangea, peonies and gypsophila in a frosted vase.

selecting the
readings

Having a religious ceremony means that you follow a more traditional format, and you are required by law to perform some vows at most civil ceremonies.

Increasingly, couples like to include a prayer, poem or reading that is very special to them to personalize the traditional ceremony. This is also a good way of involving your family members. These can be very well-known pieces of literature or poems, or creative couples can write their own. For church services one of the most popular readings is Psalm 23, 'The Lord is my Shepherd', or 1 Corinthians 13, 'The Greatest of these is love'. Popular poems include Elizabeth Barrett Brownings 'How Do I Love Thee?' or William Shakespeare's 'Sonnet 18'. A civil ceremony gives you more freedom to be informal and write your own wedding vows. However, couples who opt for a licensed venue rather than a religious ceremony often adopt the traditional church etiquette. Readings at civil weddings should be non-religious.

Your readings choices and possible readers

Readings: ....

....

....

Prayers: ....

....

....

Poems: ....

....

....

Extracts: ....

....

....

OPPOSITE Trailing and berried ivy, with 'Gracia' roses, sweet peas, eustoma, rosemary and ranunculus.
ABOVE A Victorian nosegay of grape hyacinths, 'Vendela' roses, sweet peas and forget-me-nots.

planning your
transport

Travelling to your wedding in a vintage car or in a horse-drawn carriage is traditional. The style of your wedding will dictate the type of transport you choose.

Apart from budget restraints, you will need to think of the practical issues, such as getting in and out of the car with a wedding gown on. Open-top cars look very appealing, but play havoc with your hair. One car is usually hired with a driver to deliver the bride to the ceremony with whoever is giving her away. After the ceremony the bride and groom use the car to drive to the reception. A second car is often hired to take the bridesmaids and the mother of the bride to the church or ceremony.

● Make sure you see the vehicle and meet with your driver before you book.

● Sometimes car-hire firms decorate the vehicles with flowers and ribbons, or you can ask your florist to do so.

● If the location of the wedding does not have easy parking, you may consider hiring a coach for your guests.

● If you are getting married in a remote place, it is a good idea to send detailed maps to guests and also place clear signs on the roads to guide guests on the day.

● Traditionally, at the end of the day the bride and groom leave in a decorated car. In the UK the custom is to decorate it with tin cans, balloons and streamers and a sign saying 'Just Married'.

ABOVE A London Karma Kab based on a vintage Indian Ambassador car of the 1950s.

Your transport requirements

List the different journeys you will need transport for, the people
involved and the timings.

The Reception

finding a
venue

Popular venues get booked 18 months in advance and so you may have to be flexible about your choice of date or be prepared to plan well in advance. If the ceremony is not on site, you need to choose a venue that is not more than 30 minutes away from the ceremony.

Historic homes may have restrictions, so it is a good idea to make sure you know all about these before you book. Often they are also open to the public, so you need to know your time constraints. Some monitor noise levels after a certain time, ban stiletto heels, veto flowers with heavy pollen, such as oriental lilies, or have restrictions on young children. The most common ban is naked flames, so you will have to settle for battery-operated candles and votives.

Some venues will offer you an in-house caterer or will suggest recommended suppliers. Sometimes the listed suppliers have to give a percentage of their total fee to the venue for the recommendation, and if you want to bring in a outside firm you may have to pay a surcharge. This is fairly common practice among museums and most historic venues, so it is often hard to re-negotiate this. It will inevitably add to the final cost of your wedding. Sometimes you are able to purchase the wine yourself and your caterer will serve it but charge you a corkage fee. It is important to think about parking and toilet facilities. Ideally you want one WC per 40 people. A private loo for the bride is a luxury, but something else to consider if the bride is changing and does not have a changing room on site!

'If you have a favourite restaurant as a couple, this might be your perfect venue for your wedding reception. You already know how good the food is and restaurants are generally happy to work out a bespoke menu with you as well as a personalized wine list. You know you and your guests will be comfortable, and as everything is in situ there is no need to worry about the linen and the chairs turning up!'

Roger Pizey, executive head chef of Marco Restaurant

ABOVE A giant candelabra adorned with delphiniums, peonies, garden roses and stephanotis trails.
OPPOSITE Massed balls of 'Reagan White' chrysanthemums adorn an outdoor wedding table.

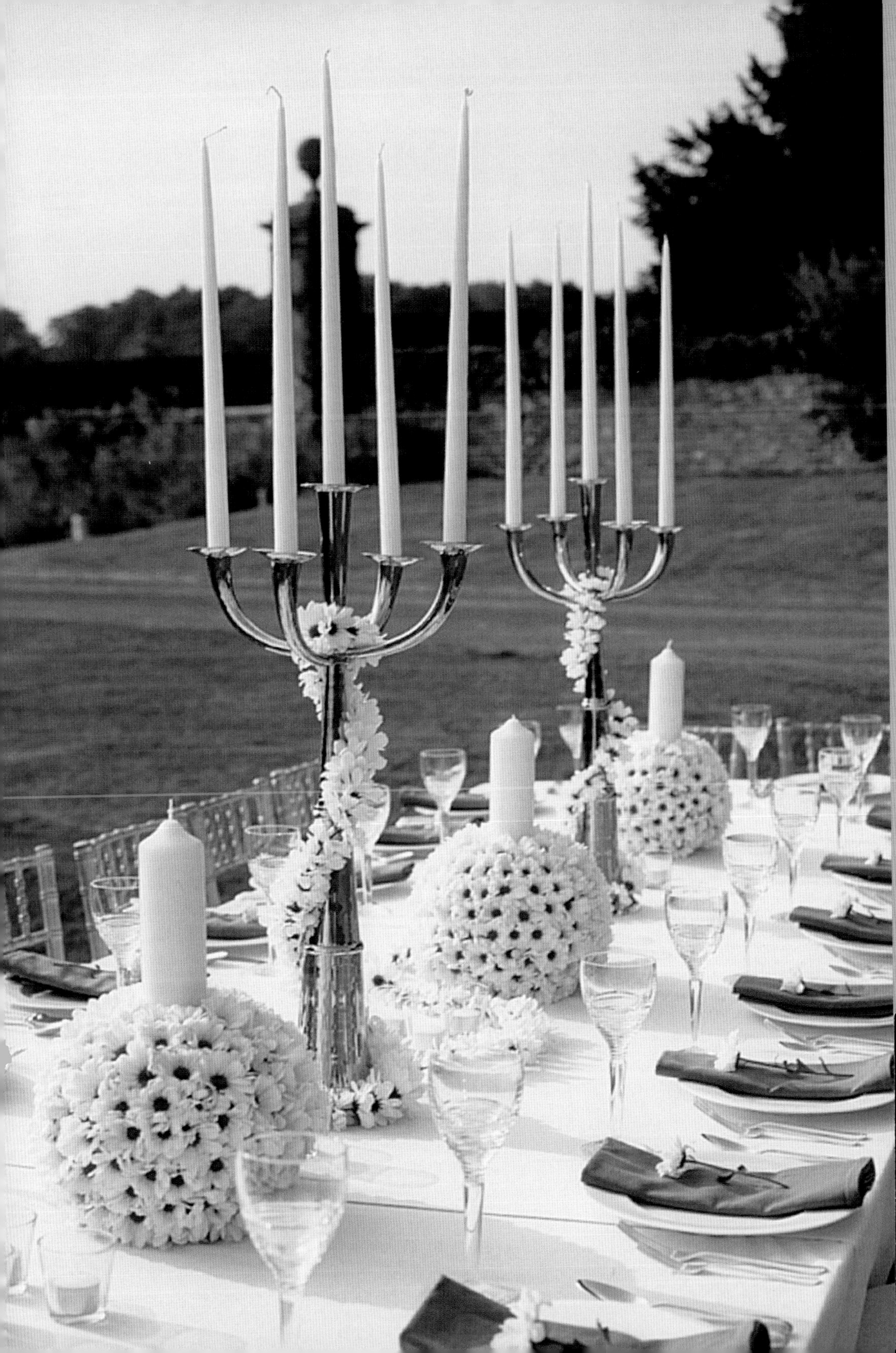

Incorporating marquees

A marquee provides a blank canvas and it is one of my favourite venues to decorate. They vary a lot in price and standard, so you will need to talk to a number of companies until you find your ideal supplier. The summer is a busy time for marquee companies and so you need to book this at least 6 months before your wedding.

If you are placing the marquee in a lovely garden or attaching it to a historic house, try to make the marquee blend in and enhance the setting. Your marquee expert will know how big you need to make the tent to carry your number of guests. They will need a visit to measure up and see the site.

Your marquee expert will be able to help you with hiring floors, staging, furniture and power in addition to the lining and lighting features. A separate catering tent is always essential.

If you choose a number of different suppliers, it is always a good idea to have one site meeting with them all so they can work together to create the effect you desire. This is common practice for your suppliers and they will be used to liaising with one another.

ABOVE A tall pedestal of pink and green hydrangea, cream and pink delphiniums, roses and scented lilies.
OPPOSITE An exotic selection of leucospermums, viburnum berries, cotinus, celosia, *Germini gerberas*, gloriosa and 'Milano', 'Orange Juice', 'Wow' and 'Supergreen' roses.

Scouting venues

Use this space to make notes as you visit different locations. Try to keep a score of how you rate each one, jotting down pros and cons. This will help you make your final decision.

Confirmed venue: ....

Contact details: ....

Confirmed timings: ....

OPPOSITE Flowering cherry and pink gypsophila are set off by a ring of 'Sweet Akito' roses, ivy berries and ranunculus.

selecting your
food

Sharing good food and wine with family and friends is key to the wedding celebration. Excellent presentation and good service are the essential factors in making the day a great success. It is always best to keep the food seasonal and simple and of the highest quality for the budget you have set. There are many catering companies and a huge variation in quality and service.

- Your caterer will suggest menu options and advise on all the practicalities of the day. When a menu has been settled on, the caterer can give you a quote.

- Often you can also have a tasting, where you will have a sample of the food on offer for your special day.

- Generally, there are three options for the reception: canapés and drinks, a buffet, a formal seated meal or a combination of these. Less formal options are a hog roast or barbecue.

- Your caterer will also be able to hire in any furniture you require, and of course will be responsible for the look of the tables. There will be many options for china, glassware and cutlery. An experienced caterer will guide you through the range of choices.

- You need to find out if any of your guests have allergies or any special dietary requirements.

- It is essential that there are enough waiting staff and generally for a formal meal you need one waiter or waitress to every 15 guests. It is also important to check what the staff will be wearing so that they coordinate with your style.

- If you intend to party late, it is always a good idea to offer some food to your guests in the latter stages.

- You will also need to feed all the staff working on your event, so they will need to be included in the final head count.

OPPOSITE A table candelabra decorated with ruscus, eucalyptus, variegated ivy and garden roses.

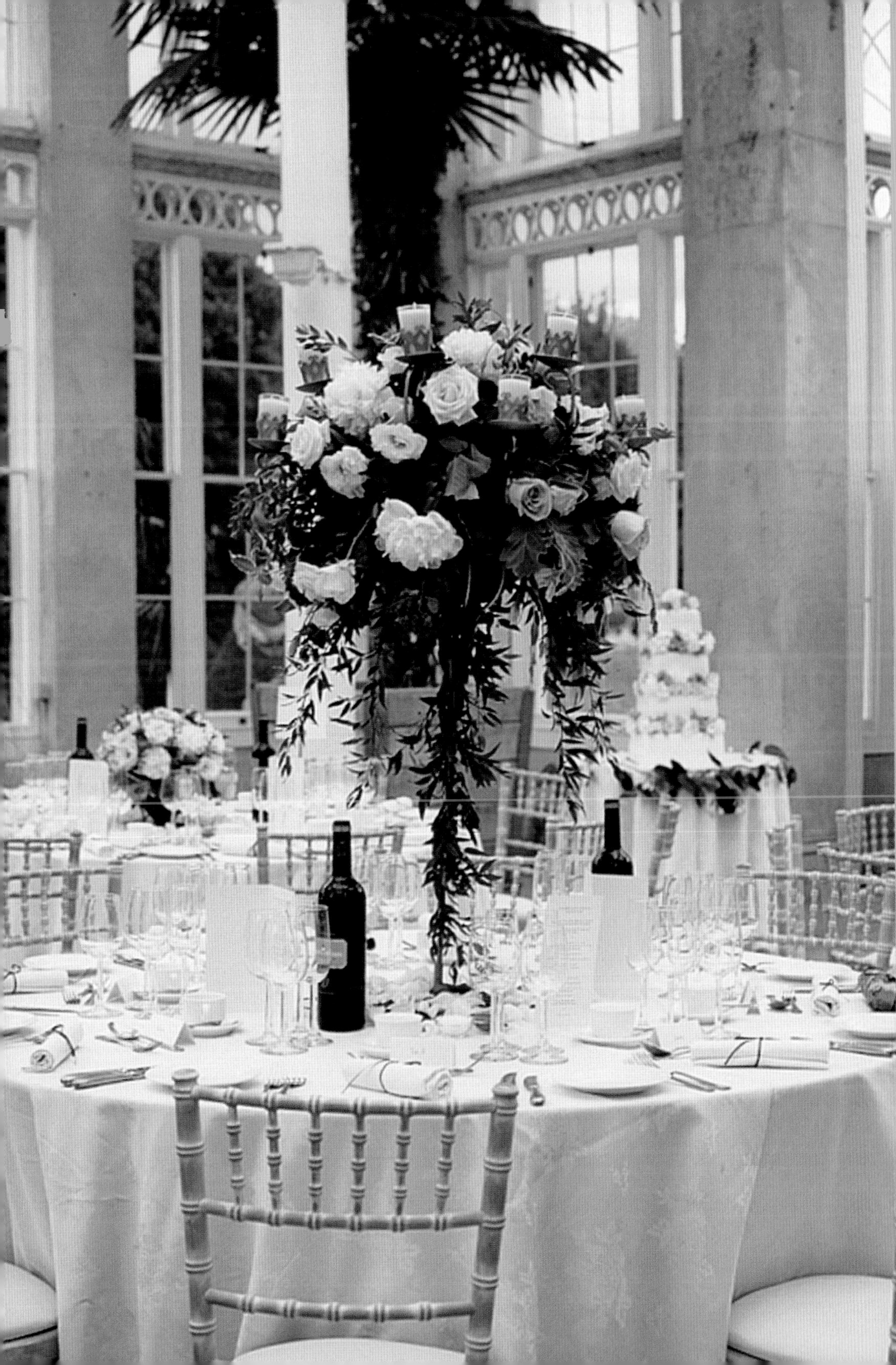

'Keep the food simple, preferably local and definitely seasonal. Have sophisticated canapés to replace the first course. It sets the tone and saves on crockery and cutlery.'

Pauline Milbank, chef and caterer

THIS PAGE A wire basket lined
with carpet moss is topped with
Dianthus 'Monica Wyatt', carnations,
chrysanthemums, asters, feverfew,
Alchemilla mollis and eustoma.

THE RECEPTION   69

Your dining choices

Make a note of how you are planning to feed your guests:
canapés, full sit-down meal, evening buffet, etc.

....

....

....

....

....

....

....

....

Confirmed caterer:..

Contact details: ....

Confirmed menus: ....

....

'Always think about your guests' dietary needs and ask for any requests from your guests way in advance. Vegetarians, vegans, lactose intolerance, wheat allergies – the list can be endless but can save any embarrassing situations on the day.'

Richard Cubbin, director of food at Allison Price Catering

Alternatives for special dietary requirements:

ABOVE   A hand-tied bouquet of cotinus, *Alchemilla mollis*, hydrangea, lilies, trailing amaranthus and gloriosa. Tall glass vases are great for tables in barns and banqueting houses. They create impact and your guests can still see each other across the table.

choosing
the drink

Drink is the essential ingredient to any celebration. The quality and the types provided will be determined by your budget and style.

● Traditionally, Champagne is essential for the toast and is served with canapés at the beginning of the reception.

● As well as alcoholic drinks, it is important to offer lots of water and non-alcoholic options. Fruit cocktails are very popular for summer weddings.

● Your caterer will provide the drinks, or you can buy them yourself and the caterer will then charge corkage to serve.

● If you are supplying your own alcohol, it is possible to purchase on a sale-or-return basis, which means that you won't run out of alcohol. In general, count one drink per person, per hour.

● It is important that the serving staff can inform your guests of the drinks available. It is best to keep the choices simple, and your caterer will need this information to pass on to the waiting staff.

● If you are having a late-night party, you might consider hiring a bar and bar tenders. You need one bar tender for every 50 guests. Cocktails can be more economical than wine as you get 18–20 drinks from a 750ml bottle of spirits compared to 5–6 glasses from a bottle of wine.

ABOVE Mixed coloured roses in votive glasses. OPPOSITE A hand-tied bouquet of dahlias, 'Con Amore', 'Cool Water', 'Blue Pacific' and 'Christian' roses, with foliage of *Heuchera* 'Plum Pudding' and *Cotinus coggygria* 'Palace Purple'.

'Wine and champagne are wonderful for weddings, but creating a signature cocktail creates a lasting memory, something you will always have, something you can mix up long after the wedding is over and continue to celebrate your special day!'
Tony Abou-Ganim, mixologist

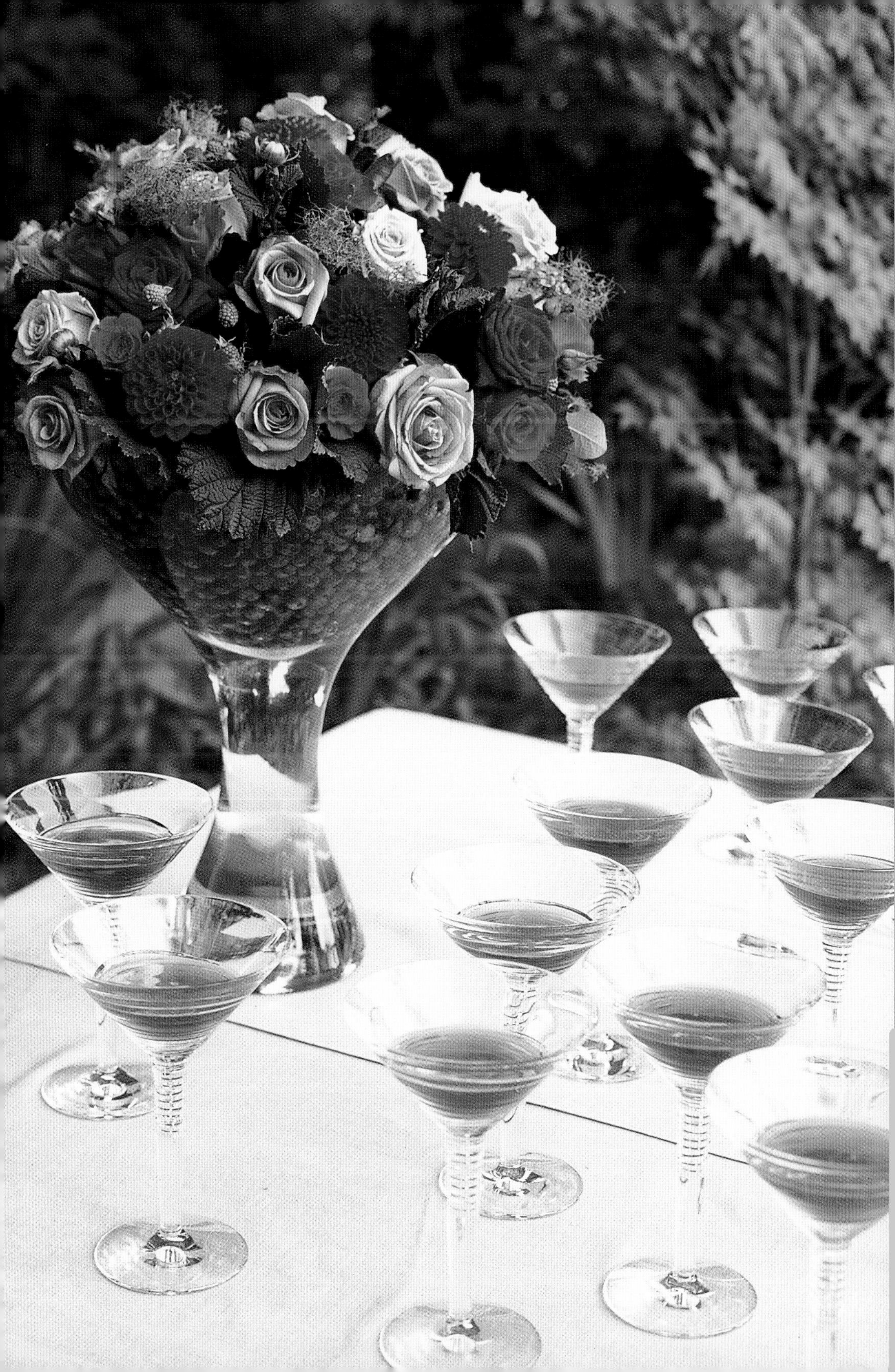

Drinks choices

List your drinks requirements and quantities here, including any welcoming drinks and aperitifs, wine with the meal, Champagne for toasts, cocktails and drinks for the evening party. Remember to include soft drink choices as well as alcoholic ones.

OPPOSITE Posies of three roses in galax leaves with a twist of decorative wire.

choosing
the cake

The wedding cake is the focal point of the reception and provides everyone with a photo opportunity.

● Traditionally, the wedding cake was a fruit cake, but now couples often chose to have one tier of fruit cake and the others to be flavoured sponge or chocolate.

● If you don't want to have a traditional wedding cake you can have a tower of mini-desserts instead. A croquembouche is also an option; this is a pyramid of profiteroles held together by molten sugar. Recently, towers of cupcakes have also proved very popular.

● If you don't have a sweet tooth, you can do the same with individual cheeses and make a similar feature.

● Cakes are usually delivered to the venue by the cake maker and set up on site. If you are having floral decorations on or round the base of the cake, you will need to ask your florist to liaise with your cake maker.

'Choose different flavours for each tier of your wedding cake. This way you will be sure to have a selection to suit all tastes. Or you could send your bridesmaids on a cake-decorating masterclass to make, bake and decorate your wedding cake for you – if you are an "anything goes" bride.'

Mich Turner, Little Venice Cake Company

OPPOSITE A three-tier cake layered with 'Blushing Akito', 'Belle Rose', 'Heaven!', 'Aqua!' and 'Lyveria!' standard roses and 'Magic Pepita' spray roses.

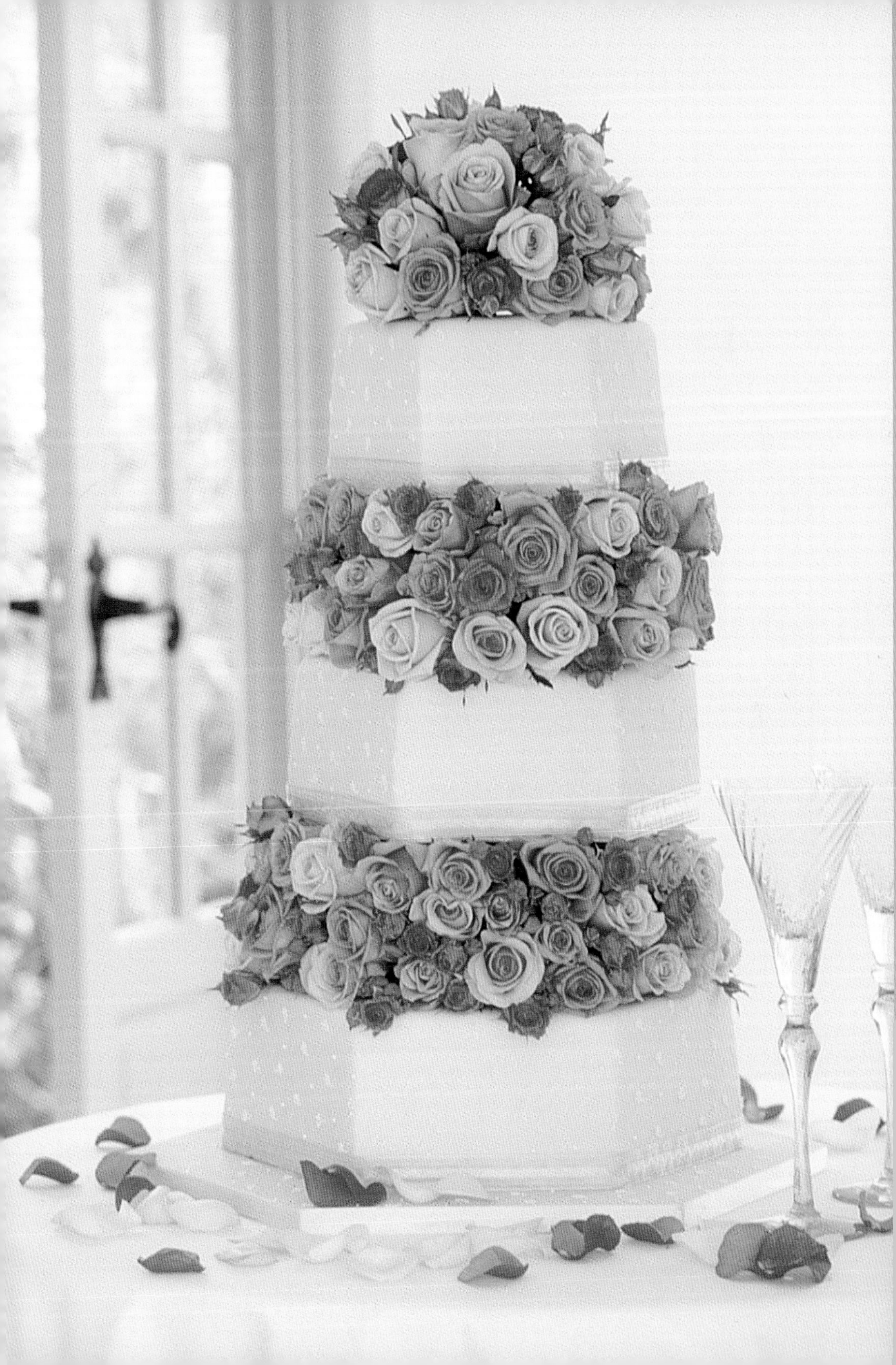

● You will also need to advise your caterer about the cake, as they will need to order a small table for this. The silver server and the knife can be provided by either the caterer or the cake maker, but the table is definitely in the caterer's remit.

● When cutting the cake, the groom should place his right hand on the bride's right hand. They make the cut together, and the bride takes the first bite and then hands the piece to the groom.

● There is a custom to send a piece of the wedding cake in a small decorated box to those who are unable to attend on the day.

THIS PAGE A ring of 'Rosita Vendella', 'Dolce Vita' and 'Barbie' roses and pink hydrangea surrounds a striped cake.

Which cake is right for you?

Make a note of which cake styles and shapes you like to get your ideas together:

Confirmed cake maker:

Contact details:

Confirmed cake design:

Delivery date and place:

planning
the entertainment

This is a vital ingredient for any wedding day to create the
party mood.

● If you are thinking about hiring a band, it is essential for the bride and groom
to see them play live. Most bands will provide you with a demo CD, but it is
always advisable to see them in action.

● Often your venue can suggest good bands that appeal to a range of guest
ages and tastes. Ideally, the band should appeal to the whole party and, of
course, you will have to notify them of any special requests you may have, such
as your first dance.

● All bands come with their own expectations and requests and their rigging,
staging and lighting costs are going to add to your costs. They will also need to
be fed and often require payment on the day.

● It is a good idea to have your band set up and practise before your guests
arrive, but sometimes this is not practical.

● It is important to determine how long they will play and to discuss the
potential of overtime if on the day you don't want the party to end! Check also
about their breaks and what recorded music will be played during these.

● Most venues have an entertainment licence, but you need to liaise with the
band and your event/location coordinator.

● If you are going for entertainment in a big way, you might approach an event
production company to advise you and to provide all the staging and lighting.

● If you are hiring a professional DJ, you need to discuss with them your
favourite types of music. Many have an online database of songs and can
advise on how to get the party dancing.

OPPOSITE A mossed candelabra decorated with acacia, *Stephanandra incisa* 'Crispa',
Portugal laurel, roses, astilbes, hydrangea and hypericum.

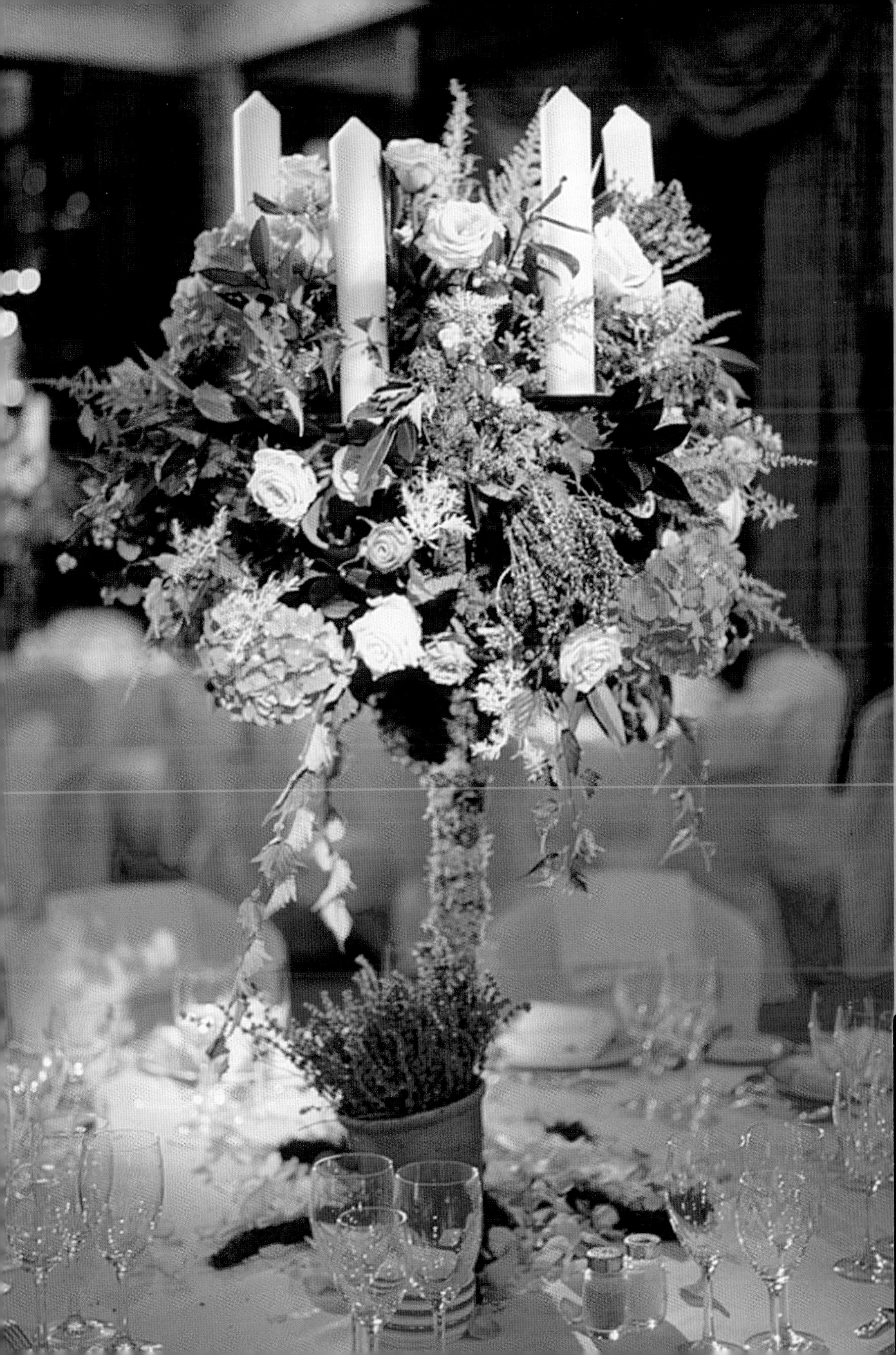

The first dance

The first dance between the bride and the groom is part of the much-anticipated etiquette of the wedding reception. Increasingly, couples take dance classes to surprise their guests and family with a beautifully choreographed dance routine. Afterwards, it is a chance for everyone to let their hair down and join in on the fun – the formal part of the wedding is over. It is also a great photo or video opportunity, as any visit to YouTube will show you!

The first dance is often after the reception, but some planners recommend slipping it in after the introductions when the couple have made their grand entrance before the wedding breakfast. Whatever song you choose, it will evoke memories for yourselves and your wedding guests for the rest of your life. Decide with your groom what dance/love songs you might consider and then discuss with your dance instructor. Remember, if you are having a live band, it may sound very different from a recorded version. Either ask your band to send you a recording of the chosen song or play the recording and get your band to join in at the end.

Remember, you don't have to do this and if it is not fun, leave this item off your to-do list. If you are not enjoying it and it's causing tensions, don't feel pressured to conform. But if you are both committed, this is also a lovely way to get fit for your wedding together, as dance is a great form of exercise and a mood enhancer!

Reception music choices

Music for the first dance: ....

Confirmed DJ: ....

Contact details: ....

....

Confirmed band: ....

Contact details: ....

....

OPPOSITE A hand-tied posy of *Achillea* 'Moonshine', zinnias, 'Colandro' and 'Milano' roses, gloriosa, celandro and cotinus.

The Guests

preparing your guest list

Traditionally, it was the bride's family who sent out the invitations, but more often nowadays it is the bride and groom themselves. It is also customary to allocate half the guests to each side of the family.

● The budget and the venue size will determine how many guests you can invite. Invitations can be the most fraught area of your wedding planning.

● Save the date cards are increasingly popular. You might want to give advance warning of the event so that you have a better chance of everyone being able to attend. These cards usually just give the date and the occasion, and the rest of the details follow with the invitation.

● It is estimated that on average 20 per cent of guests will have to decline the invitation. This is likely to be less if you have sent out save the date cards.

● Send out all the invitations about 8–12 weeks before the event and keep a list of all who have been invited. Reply cards are a good idea to enable your guests to reply easily and quickly to your invitation.

● You may also have a reserve wish list of invitees that you may release if more than anticipated numbers decline your invitation.

ABOVE White roses, nerines and hydrangea in an autumnal ring, with *Brachyglottis* 'Sunshine' on the napkin.
OPPOSITE A topiary of stephanotis, camellia, *Brachyglottis* 'Sunshine', viburnum berries, hydrangea, 'Talea', 'Metallina' and 'Old Dutch' roses and eustoma.

Managing your guest list

List your guests here as you receive your confirmations.

Guest	Contact details

Guest	Contact details

The Guests

designing your
invitations and stationery

Your wedding stationery is the first impression of your wedding. From the moment that invitation hits the doormat your celebration style is revealed.

● The classic wedding-invitation copperplate script- ideally engraved on stiff and heavy card. Originally this was 8 x 6 inches and folded with the information on the first outer page. Shape, colour, typeface and design are all things to consider.

● Often, lined envelopes or ribbons are added as finishing touches.

● Nowadays there are no set rules or etiquette about wedding stationery and a myriad of different choices, from handmade, design led or printing your own using a computer package, are available.

● Remember when deciding how many to print that you generally only need one per couple or family.

● The invitation should also include all the other information that the guest will need, including accommodation advice, a reply card (ideally with special dietary needs noted), dress code, map if necessary and parking advice. Of course you need to include the time that you plan to draw the event to a close, normally referred to as 'carriages'.

THIS PAGE AND OPPOSITE
Stephanotis sprigs and ivy berries.

'I always advise people to have small service sheet booklets (¼ A4) as they can go into pockets or handbags. When they are bigger they get left behind. Or lost under tables. We are always collecting lots of them at the end of the evening because people have not been able to get them in their bags or suit pockets.'

Wendy Milbank, caterer

Managing your stationery

	Selected	Ordered	Received
Invitations			
Order of Service			
Place markers			
Menu			
Table numbers			
Thank-you cards			

OPPOSITE A single rose in a bud vase.

The Guests

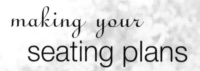

making your
seating plans

If you are having an informal reception, you may allow your guests to choose where they sit. However, if you are having a formal reception you will need to provide a seating plan. This is not an easy task and requires a good knowledge of all the guests. It is also diplomatic to discuss this with both families to get a harmonious and good result.

● The plan for the tables often gets changed, as guests can fall out, so don't leave this to the last minute. The aim is to try and out people together who know each other and enjoy each other's company. Generally, married couples are on the same tables, but not next to each other.

● Nowadays it is less common to have a formal long top table. Family splits and divorces have encouraged brides and grooms to move away from this tradition. It is also more sociable to sit at a round or oval table, rather than in a line facing the party.

● If you do decide on a formal top table the usual format is to have the bride and groom in the centre, then the groom sits next to the bride's mother and the bride sits next to her father. Bridesmaids and the best man are often included in this format. Some couples have such a complicated family structure that they opt for just a table for two!

● Usually, close family sit near the bridal party. It is customary for the bride and groom to be the last to take their places at the table so that they make a grand entrance and are applauded.

● Your event coordinator will discuss the plan of the room and the table sizes. Round tables of 1.5m (5 feet) seat 8 to 10 people, whereas the largest tables of 1.8m (6 feet) can seat 10 to 12. Your venue will give you a drawing of how the seating plan for your wedding will work.

● On the day it will be the job of your caterer or event coordinator to make sure all the place cards are in the correct spot. Once you have given them the table plan, it is down to the caterer to get the people to their right place.

● The venue will usually provide easels on which you can display your seating plan. Alternatively, you can offer alphabetically organized escort cards. These folded cards have the guest's name on the outside and the table number on the inside. Your guest can then decide where he or she sits on the designated table.

● Some couples like to theme their tables rather than have them numbered, and might choose common passions, such as mountains, racecourses or gardens.

● Don't let any family feuds or issues spoil your day. Everyone should be reunited in their love and support for you.

'Seating plans work best when they are alphabetical. Guests panic if they are ploughing through 200 names and they are not finding theirs. It also takes ages get them all settled at their table. It is also fun to have table names rather than numbers or letters. If you do have numbers and they go higher than 12, leave out 13 as some people are really superstitious.'

Wendy Milbank, caterer

OPPOSITE Birch thrones decorated with celosia, roses, asclepias, hydrangea, delphiniums and sweet peas.

The Guests

Allocating your tables

If you do decide to use place cards, you will also have to position each guest on the table, which can be a huge challenge and very time-consuming! Allowing everyone to choose their own seats at their table is less formal and often the flexibility is appreciated by your guests. Use this space to sketch out tables with your groupings of guests on each table.

choosing party favours

Traditionally, five sugared almonds were wrapped in some organza and give to each female guest at the wedding. This tradition came from Italy and the gift was known as a *bombonière*. These symbolized health, happiness, wealth, fertility and long life. Most brides now take this decorative issue very seriously and there are many companies now just specializing in making favours.

Some brides also like to show their creativity by making a handmade gift. This could be something edible, such as a biscuit or cupcake to take home, or a pot of homemade jam or marmalade. Favours can also be something like a bulb, small plant, a posy of herbs or some seeds. Scented candles or even monogrammed gifts with the bride's and groom's names are also offered as momentos of the day. Sometimes the favours are also offered to men.

I think the most successful favours are ones that contain a local original gift; a pot of honey or handmade confectionary are good ideas. Children often receive packs to play with or little games they can play. Bear in mind that this adds to the costs and also the workload. The bride and groom should consider if this is necessary or if they have the time for this extra. You may be sacrificing something that would make more impact on the overall feel and look of the day.

OPPOSITE A posy of 'Two Faces' roses.

The Guests

THIS PAGE Tightly massed 'Sarah Bernhardt' and 'Karl Rosenfeld' peonies and 'Milano', 'Belle Rose', 'Two Faces' and 'Venelle' roses. OPPOSITE A 'Lyveria!' rose.

drawing up your
wedding gift list

Most couples provide a gift list for their friends and family, and register either with a department store or online. It is normal that you should set this up around three months before the wedding date.

Gifts need to be chosen from a wide range of price points for the ease of your guests. The circumstances and the age of the bride and groom will determine the list. Some people request nothing at all. Increasingly, if couples have known each other for a long time, they may ask for something to make a new collection. It is unusual to just ask for money, although some couples do this as a donation towards their honeymoon or for future world travels.

Traditionally, the guest would contact the family to ask where the list is held, but nowadays couples send out this information with their invitations. Alternatively some brides and grooms set up websites with all the information on their wedding, including the gift list.

THIS PAGE Flowering mint, *Alchemilla mollis*, garden roses, hydrangea and lavender.

Gift list registers

List the stores here where you would like your lists held.

Gift list registered at: ....

Contact details: ....

Website access: ....

Gift list registered at: ....

Contact details: ....

Website access: ....

Gift list registered at: ....

Contact details: ....

Website access: ....

Gift list registered at: ....

Contact details: ....

Website access: ....

The Guests

The Bride

'First and foremost, keep it simple: good-quality fabric and a well-cut dress that enhances your best features. A simple dress could be complemented with a touch of whimsy, such as pastel shoes, a dramatic headpiece or a creative bouquet. I always advise brides to opt for classic, elegant styles rather than following the latest concept or trend in order to avoid the inevitable "What was I thinking?" a few years down the line. Don't overdo it and I can guarantee you will feel sensational on your big day.'

Bruce Oldfield, fashion designer

deciding on
the dress

Once you've got your date and location sorted out, the next task is to find the dress for your special day. For some the search for the perfect gown can be the most exciting part of the planning, but for others it can be the most overwhelming. The choice is immense and if you are choosing to have a handmade dress you need to a set about this task at least six months before your wedding.

● If you are not sure where to start, take a good friend or your mother to a department store to try on a range of dresses to work out what suits you and which designers you are drawn to.

● Bridal shops require appointments. Often, the assistants will be able to guide you into a style that is perfect for your body.

● Wear your best lingerie and take a strapless bra so you can see all the gowns without any distractions.

● If you are planning to wow your guests with your first dance, make sure your dress allows you to move.

● If you are torn between two gowns, always choose the more classical style. You can add an edge by having brightly coloured flowers or a dramatic bouquet.

● Once the dress has been chosen, the shop will have one tailor-made to your requirements. There may be several fittings and often last-minute adjustments, because most brides lose a little weight in the run-up to their wedding.

● Looking at magazines or attending bridal shows can be a little overwhelming, and there is no substitute for trying the gowns yourself.

● Each dress looks very different on the hanger and on a model. When you have found a dress that suits you, it will transform you into a beautiful bride.

● Above all the dress must make you feel comfortable and confident. Most women will know immediately when they have found the perfect gown.

OPPOSITE A shower-shaped bouquet of *Zantedeschia aethiopica*, a petite form of calla lily.

What's your perfect dress?

List your ideas for the style you like and designers you admire.

ABOVE A hand-tied teardrop of massed 'Shirley Temple' peonies.

Confirmed designer/shop: ....

Contact details: ....

Fittings booked for: ....

....

....

....

Accessories needed: ....

....

....

....

....

....

....

....

....

....

ABOVE Mixed garden roses.

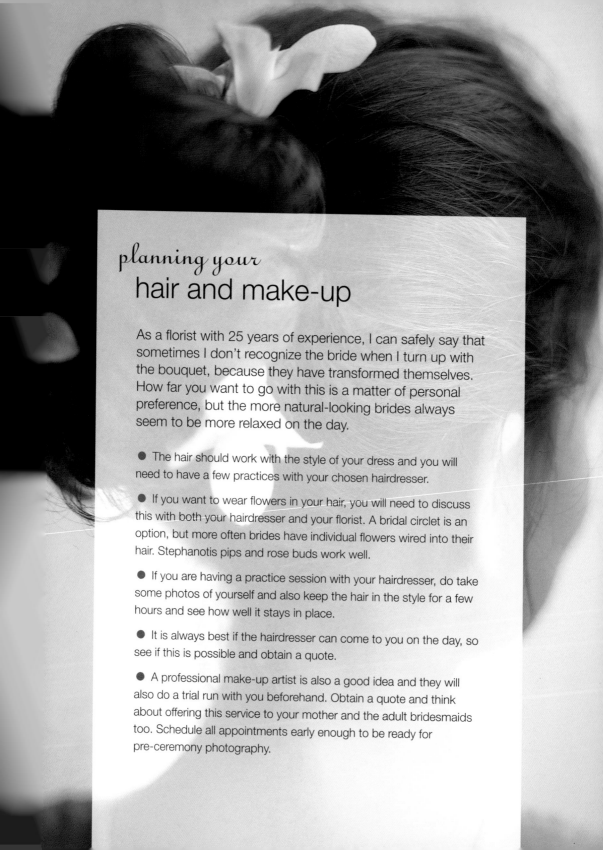

planning your
hair and make-up

As a florist with 25 years of experience, I can safely say that sometimes I don't recognize the bride when I turn up with the bouquet, because they have transformed themselves. How far you want to go with this is a matter of personal preference, but the more natural-looking brides always seem to be more relaxed on the day.

● The hair should work with the style of your dress and you will need to have a few practices with your chosen hairdresser.

● If you want to wear flowers in your hair, you will need to discuss this with both your hairdresser and your florist. A bridal circlet is an option, but more often brides have individual flowers wired into their hair. Stephanotis pips and rose buds work well.

● If you are having a practice session with your hairdresser, do take some photos of yourself and also keep the hair in the style for a few hours and see how well it stays in place.

● It is always best if the hairdresser can come to you on the day, so see if this is possible and obtain a quote.

● A professional make-up artist is also a good idea and they will also do a trial run with you beforehand. Obtain a quote and think about offering this service to your mother and the adult bridesmaids too. Schedule all appointments early enough to be ready for pre-ceremony photography.

Accessories

You only get one chance to wear a veil and certainly if you are having a religious ceremony it is a traditional accessory. Veils of lace or tulle come in many lengths. Generally, the more formal the dress, the longer the veil. These are usually secured with a band of flowers or a tiara. If you are planning to wear a veil and a headdress you need to practise all this with your hairdresser. If you are choosing to wear flowers, you need to ask your florist to make a practice headdress. There will be a charge for this, as wiring flowers is time-consuming, but it will be worth it on the day to know how it all goes together.

Bridal lingerie is also a must in order to do your gown justice. Shoes are also important – you need to make sure you have purchased all the accessories before your final dress fitting when you put the whole look together. Wear in your shoes a little before the big day so they are comfortable.

OPPOSITE *Dendrobium* 'Singapore' orchids wired and woven into the hair. ABOVE A headband of 'Tamango' roses and ivy leaves.

Booking your beauty treatments

Keep a note of the treatments you want for yourself and your bridesmaids.

	Location/supplier	Date and time
Massage		
Facial		
Eyebrow tint		
Manicure		
Pedicure		
Spray tan		
Haircut and style		
Other		

OPPOSITE A vanda orchid corsage.

choosing your
bridal bouquet

Flowers add to the beauty, scent and colour of your day. Once you have decided upon your dress, your floral designer will help you find the perfect bouquet. I love to meet brides at one of their fittings as the bridal gown completely transforms them. The flowers need to complement the dress perfectly. If it is not practical to see the bride trying on her dress, then I ask for a photo of her wearing it.

● As a general rule the more intricate and detailed the dress, the simpler the flowers should be. Overwhelmingly brides choose traditional white, but some brides use their bouquet to bring colour to the event.

● The flowers have to be in proportion to the bride's height and size and also to the dress. The shape of the bouquet – round or a trailing – will be determined by the style of the gown.

● Princess gowns, ball gowns and bias-cut gowns suit longer shower bouquets. A fishtail or trumpet shape may also suggest a more dramatic flower selection. A-line, column, sheath and tea-length dresses look great with round bouquets. Your florist will advise you, as the type and shade of the fabric will also suggest what flowers will work best.

● Other important factors will be the time of year, the setting and the length of the event. Some flowers are more sturdy than others, and popular choices such as lily of the valley and sweet peas don't do well in the heat of full summer.

● One aspect to consider is having some scented flowers. If possible, I always think it is lovely to include some fragrance. However, bear in mind that all scented flowers are usually more fragile than non-scented varieties.

● The main choice is whether to have a natural hand-tied bouquet or whether to have a wired bouquet. Wired bouquets allow for the florist to make a linear or a more intricate design. Traditionally, all bouquets were wired, but in the last 25 years there has been an increase in natural-stemmed bouquets. Wiring flowers takes longer and is more time-consuming, so there will be a cost implication. Whichever you decide on, your florist can cover the stems or handle with some wedding silk or satin ribbon.

● My favourite flower choices for bridal bouquets are roses, peonies, ranunculus, lily of the valley, sweet peas and orchids.

OPPOSITE A hand-tied bouquet of veronica, *Alchemilla mollis*, echinops, 'Sarah Bernhardt' peonies, scabious, 'Cool Water!' roses and amaranthus.

What kind of bouquet?

The most popular shape of bridal bouquet is round. Flowers can be arranged on the natural stems or, if more delicate, they will need to be wired. The pipped stephanotis is a wired bouquet, while the rest shown here are on natural stems. Teardrops or long shower bouquets all require the flowers to be wired, so this will add to the time and cost of your bouquet. Most often a round or teardrop shape photographs best.

TOP ROW, LEFT TO RIGHT A wired bouquet of scented stephanotis. Muscari, 'Sweet Akito' roses, *Astilbe* 'Erica' and blue nigella. 'Akito' roses hand-tied with *Bouvardia* 'Diamond White'. BOTTOM ROW, LEFT TO RIGHT White peonies edged with hosta leaves. A dome of mixed garden roses, *Viburnum opulus* and *Astrantia major*. Massed lily of the valley. *Zantedeschia* 'Aurora', 'Talea' roses and *Astilbe* 'Erica'.

Your bouquet

Confirmed florist: ....

Contact details: ....

Confirmed bouquet: ....

....

....

....

Delivery date, time and place: ....

....

....

....

....

....

....

....

....

....

OPPOSITE A heart-shaped bouquet of 'Sweet Akito' roses.
ABOVE 'Vendela' roses, ranunculus, muscari and *Bouvardia* 'Pink Diamond'.

The Bridal Party

picking your
bridal party

As soon as you start to put the wedding together, you need to select your bridal party. A good team of reliable close friends can really make the day run smoothly. The important positions are the chief bridesmaid and the best man. These are the two that you need to delegate to, and who will be looking out for you on your big day.

The bridegroom needs to choose some groomsmen or ushers and the bride chooses some bridesmaids and page boys. How many you choose is up to you, but of course the larger the bridal party, the bigger the budget needed.

A meeting with all the adult team is advised ahead of the stag and hen nights (bachelor/bachelorette parties). Make sure everyone knows what you expect of them. A rehearsal is also beneficial, so that everything runs smoothly on the day. The biggest role goes to the best man, who usually has to make sure the whole schedule keeps to time and all the guests are taken care of.

ABOVE The bridal party carrying classic nosegays of white sweet peas. OPPOSITE The bouquets include 'Blue Curiosa', 'Blue Gene', 'Sterling Silver and 'Avalanche' roses, with *Viburnum opulus*.

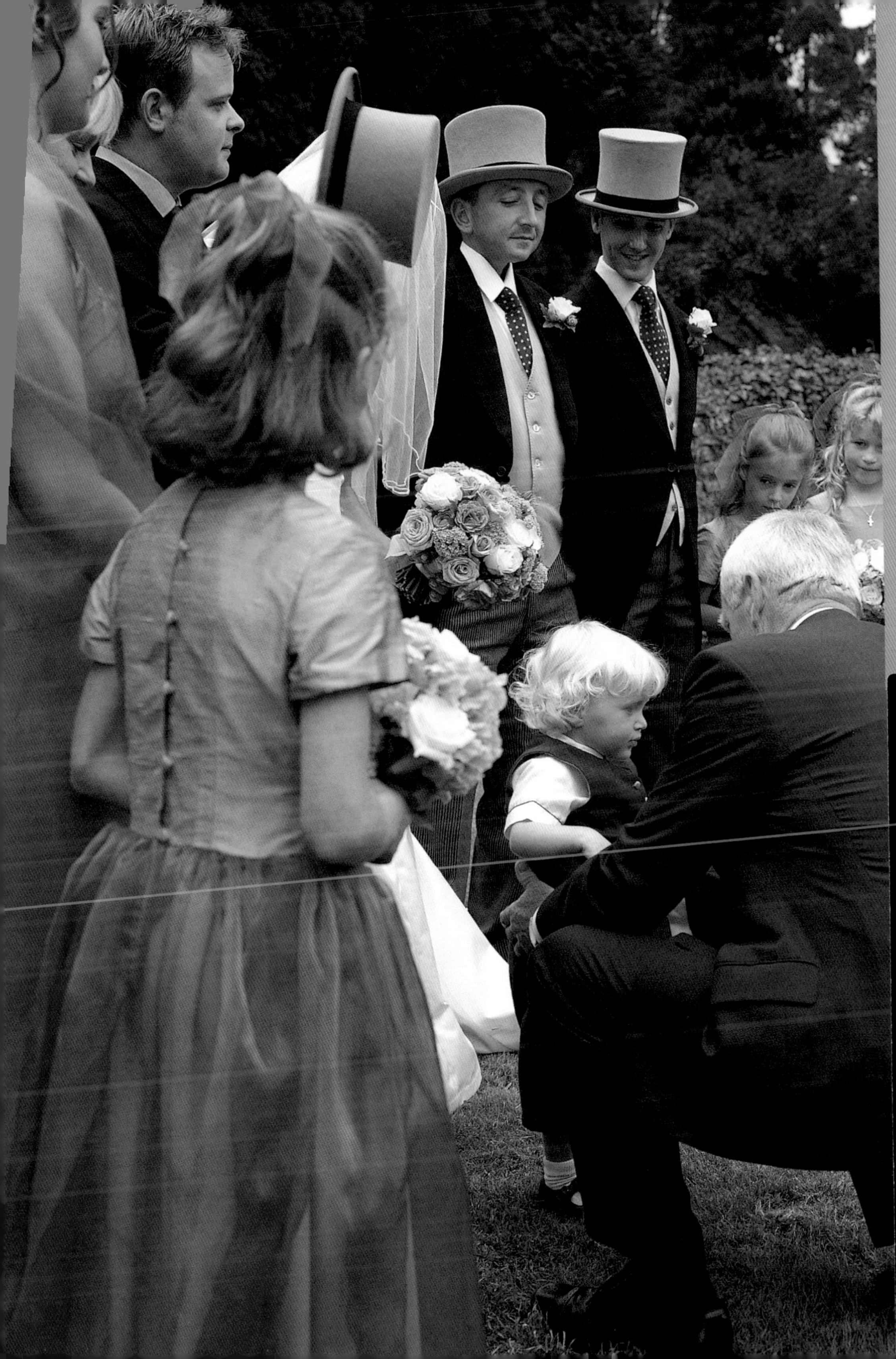

choosing the
wardrobe for the day

After a dress code is set, it is customary for the bride and groom to pay for the hire or purchase of the suits and dresses of the bridal party. Usually, the male attire is hired, but sometimes ties and waistcoats (vests) are specially made. If the wedding is before noon, it is traditional to wear a formal morning suit in grey or black. Later weddings can call for a tuxedo or Black Tie. If you hire suits for the event, delegate someone to return them all after your wedding when you will be on honeymoon. The best man would be a perfect choice. Cream linen suits are an option for outdoor parties. Bridesmaids' dresses are usually purchased, and coordinating the shoes is also an important consideration. There are many bespoke wedding shoe designers, and shoe-dying services offer you the chance to match shoes to the dresses.

ABOVE A buttonhole (boutonniére) of *Eucharis amazonica*. OPPOSITE A white peony bouquet edged with hosta leaves is simple but elegant.

Bridal party wardrobe

List your bridal party wardrobe requirements here.

Groom: ....

....

....

....

Best man: ....

....

....

....

Bridesmaids: ....

....

....

....

....

....

....

Groomsmen/ushers: ....

....

....

....

Flower girls/page boys: ....

....

....

....

....

Parents of the bride and groom: ....

....

....

....

....

....

....

....

selecting the
bridal party flowers

Once you have chosen a colour for your wedding, this will influence the choice of flowers you pick.

● It is customary for each bridesmaid to have a round bouquet and sometimes a headband of fresh flowers. Even if the bride holds a white or ivory bouquet, you can bring out the colour of the wedding through these flowers.

● Small bridesmaids or flower girls have smaller posies, hold baskets, handbags of flowers or even a round pomander. Children under the age of three do find it very difficult to hold flowers or wear them. You might consider a small rosebud to wear or even a wrist corsage.

● The bridegroom will have a buttonhole that matches the bride's bouquet, and very often the ushers will have something similar.

● Roses are overwhelmingly the most chosen flower for buttonholes, usually trimmed with some herbs or berries.

ABOVE A bridesmaid's pomander of 'N-joy' roses. OPPOSITE, CLOCKWISE FROM TOP LEFT A basket of *Sanguisorba officinalis* 'Pink Tanna', rue and *Tanecetum parthenium* 'Pure Kamille'. A single rose bud in a metal corsage holder. *Chrysanthemum* 'Reagan White' in a terracotta pot. A hand-tied posy of 'Barcelona' tulips.

Bridal party flowers

List your confirmed bridal party flower requirements here.

....

....

....

....

....

....

....

....

....

Delivery date, time and place: ....

....

....

....

....

....

OPPOSITE, CLOCKWISE FROM TOP LEFT *Phalaenopsis* orchid with lily grass loops. 'Bianca' rose with *Eryngium planum* 'Blue Candle', 'Vendela' rose edged with camellia leaves and ivy berries. Gloriosa with grass loops and wire binding.

bridal party
thank-you gifts

It is customary to give a small gift to all the bridal party for helping you, and it is down to the best man on the day to make sure that this happens. Often he will toast the bridesmaids and then presents will be awarded. It is also the custom to have bouquets or gifts for the mother of the bride and the mother of the bridegroom.

Traditions vary a lot and increasingly the thank-yous are part of the rehearsal dinner the night before, in more intimate surroundings. The American tradition is also to fill a themed guest basket for hotel guests, or include a handwritten welcome from the bride and groom.

Your thank-you gift list...

ABOVE A hand-tied bouquet of 'Anna' roses. OPPOSITE Garden roses and *Sanguisorba officinalis* 'Pink Tanna'.

Your Record
of the Day

the best ways of
remembering the day

The day will pass so fast that you will be glad to have a record so you can relive this emotional event. Disposable cameras were all the rage for a while, and more recently these have been surpassed by inexpensive digital cameras. The new trend is to have a photo booth where you set up an additional fun area to have all your guests recorded. This can be themed for all ages.

A lovely handmade guest book is also a great way to record the day. Your guests will all write a special wish for you. Some couples have a wish tree, designed by their floral designer, for guests to pin notes onto. Some brides and grooms get very creative with this idea. If you have guests coming from all over the world, you could have a huge map on which people can mark where they live and write their comments as a keepsake.

ABOVE 'Daily Star' chrysanthemums, 'Duchesse de Nemo' and 'Green Planet' roses, hydrangea, *Viburnum tinus* and *Alchemilla mollis*. OPPOSITE Autumnal table candelabras of dahlias and hydrangea with trailing amaranthus.

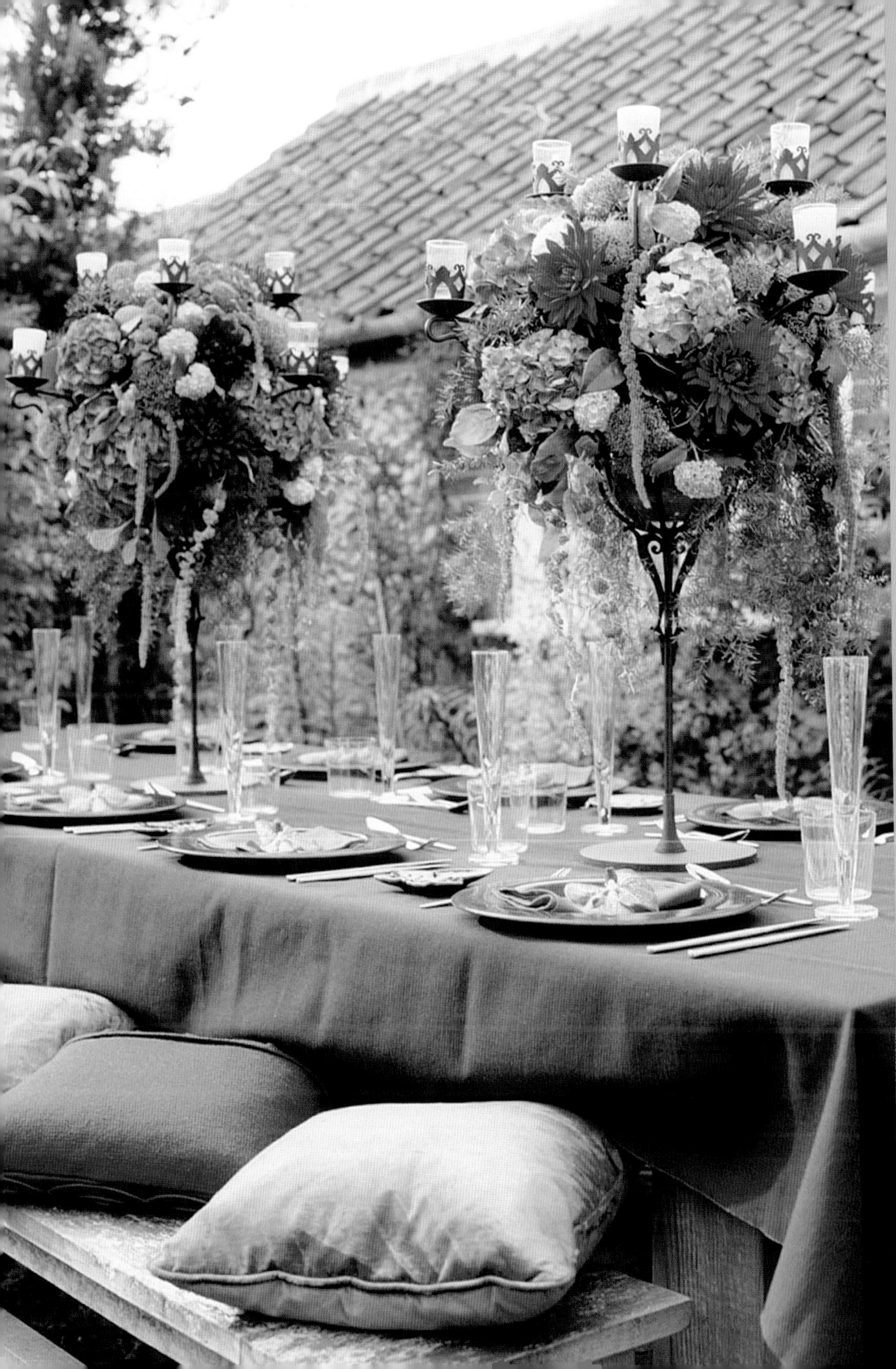

picking a
photographer

There are so many styles of photography to choose from and also many different scales of pay. Pick a photographer whose work you like and who you will be happy to share the day with. Like most areas of your wedding, you get what you pay for, and talented wedding photographers get booked way in advance. This is not an area you can leave to the latter planning stages.

Secure your photographer with a contract early. Increasingly, wedding photographers work in a team of two so they can get everything recorded. Provide your photographer with a written shot list so that there can be no misunderstandings about what you want photographed. Generally, people plump for more formal pictures at the beginning of the day and more reportage style for the end of the celebration.

'Firstly, don't book a photographer if you don't like their photos; there is no point in booking someone and then asking him or her to change what they do. Second, you have to actually like the photographer and agree with the way they tend to do things. Ask them to explain their approach to the day and make sure it matches yours. Choose someone that you like and that you know will fit in with your family and friends. After the wedding, the last thing you want to say is, "We love our wedding photos, but . . ." There should never be a "but"!'

Damian Bailey, photographer

OPPOSITE 'Gertude Jekyll', 'Prima Donna' and 'Super Green' roses, *Alchemilla mollis*, nigella, nerines, campanula and 'Sarah Bernhardt' peonies.

choosing a
videographer

A film is a great record of your day that you can look back on and share with your family. Nothing captures the essence of the day like cinematic film. Prices vary enormously and remember that a great film is all in the cut, and so the more time the videographer spends on the film, the better the production.

Look at your videographer's show reels to interview them. You can personalize your own video with music from your wedding and favourite tunes. Sometimes you can hire photographers and videographers from the same company, which can be helpful as they will need to liaise and work together. Ideally, you need them to have a slightly different focus so you get the full benefits of having both working for you.

In recent years video montages have become very popular. This is a record of the lives of the groom and bride from birth to the engagement photos. Sometimes these are played at the reception or for the rehearsal dinner.

OPPOSITE A dog collar of 'Grand Prix' roses, skimmia and hydrangea. BELOW Wildflower arrangements of ox-eye daisies, scabious and *Alchemilla mollis* with wheat in vintage earthenware pickling jars.

THIS PAGE Hydrangea, lilies and
roses top freestanding candelabras.

Your photographer and videographer

Confirmed photographer: ....

Contact details: ....

Details of shots agreed: ....

....

....

....

....

....

Confirmed timings: ....

....

Confirmed videographer: ....

Contact details: ....

Details of coverage agreed: ....

....

....

....

....

Confirmed timings: ....

your wishes for
the future

After the build-up to the big day, the following day can feel quite emotional and anticlimactic. It is a natural reaction to all the stress of planning a wedding and then being the centre of a huge amount of love and attention on the day.

It is also a shock to a lot of couples how quickly everything gets dismantled and removed. You've spent months planning this day, and when you leave all your suppliers start to work on the 'strike' of your event, taking everything down and removing it ready for the next one.

Never lose sight of the original reason why you chose to get married. Focus on this new and happy phase of your life together. Try not to place the wedding event above your relationship. Now you can really start to plan your future life together.

ABOVE Peonies, dahlias, sweet peas, *Alchemilla mollis* and vines of *Clematis montana*.
OPPOSITE *Viburnum opulus* 'Roseum', roses and ivy foliage.

recording your
memories of the day

Record your thoughts on your wedding day. Try to do this immediately afterwards while memories are still fresh, even if they are just snapshots of the day.

OPPOSITE A Victorian posy of 'Winterberg' tulips, 'Alexis' roses, *Narcissus tazetta* 'Avalanche', twisted willow, muscari and fritillaria.

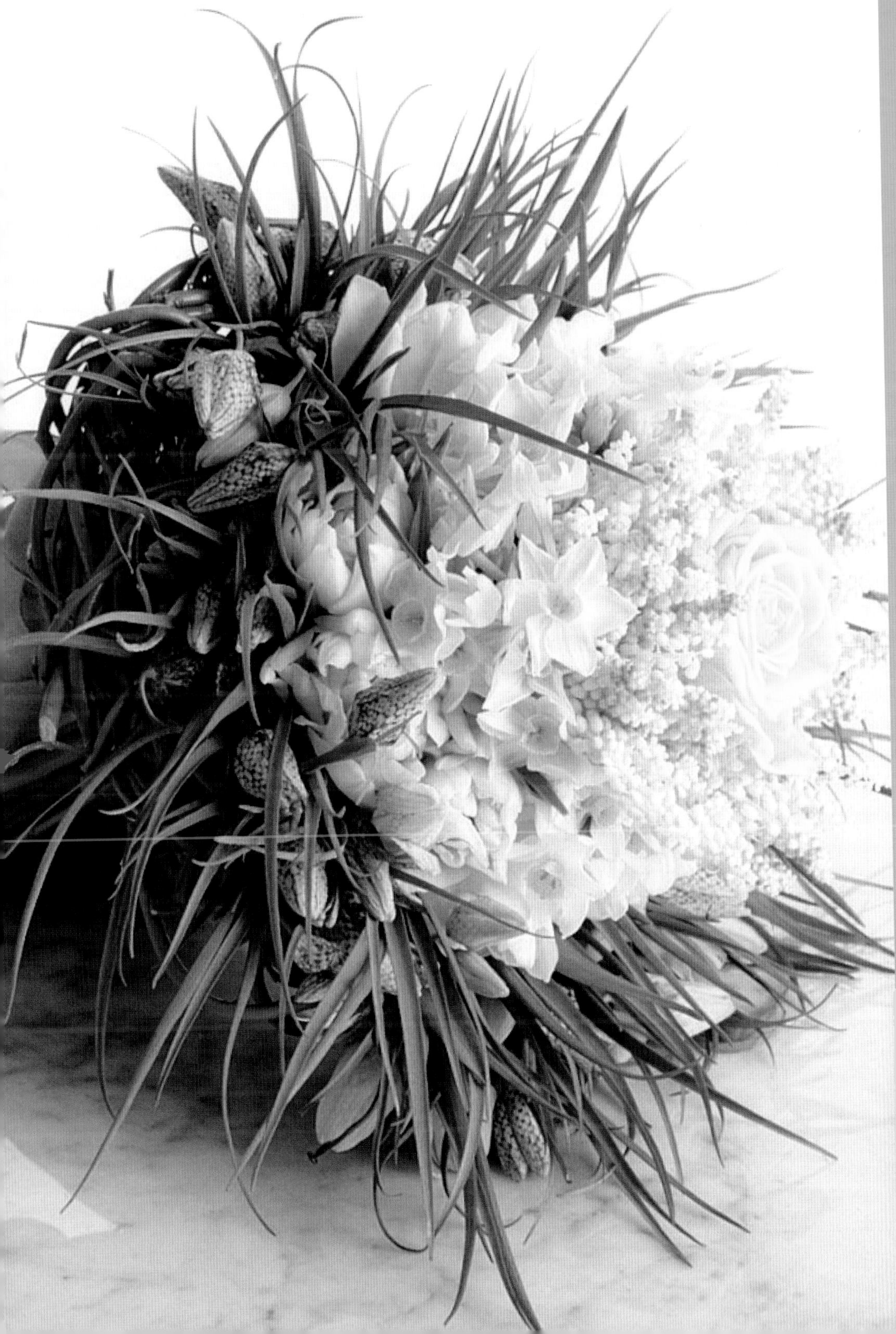

Address Book

Key contacts

Use this section to keep all your contact information in one place, so you can access it easily.

Company

Contact ....

Numbers ....

....

Email/website ....

Company

Contact ....

Numbers ....

....

Email/website ....

Company

Contact ....

Numbers ....

....

Email/website ....

Company

Contact ....

Numbers ....

....

Email/website ....

Company

Contact

Numbers

Email/website

Company

Contact

Numbers

Email/website

Company

Contact

Numbers

Email/website

Company

Contact

Numbers

Email/website

Address Book

Key contacts

Company

Contact

Numbers

Email/website

Company

Contact

Numbers

Email/website

Company

Contact

Numbers

Email/website

Company

Contact

Numbers

Email/website

Company

Contact

Numbers

Email/website

Company

Contact

Numbers

Email/website

Company

Contact

Numbers

Email/website

Company

Contact

Numbers

Email/website

Recommended suppliers of wedding services

Accessories
www.butlerandwilson.co.uk
www.rainbowclub.co.uk
www.gillianmillion.com
www.pollyedwards.com
www.wrightandteague.com
www.hermioneharbutt.com
www.brittenweddings.co.uk

Bridal Gowns
www.neilcunningham.com
www.phillipalepley.com
www.ritvawestenius.com
www.sassiholford.com
www.sophie-english.co.uk
www.verawang.com
www.valentino.com
www.brownsfashion.com
www.stewartparvin.com
www.morgandavieslondon.co.uk
www.jennypackham.com
www.marchesa.co.uk
www.bruceoldfield.com
www.thevintageweddingdresscompany.com

Bridesmaids
www.littlebevan.co.uk
www.nickimacfarlane.com
www.ghost.co.uk
www.twobridesmaids.co.uk
www.littleeglantine.com
www.lila-lila.com
www.ilovegorgeous.co.uk

Cakes
www.thecakeparlour.com
www.patacakepatacake.com
www.chocolateweddingcakes.co.uk
www.choccywoccydoodah.com
www.konditorandcook.com
www.lvcc.co.uk
www.peggyporschen.com
www.cakesbykrishanthi.co.uk
www.rosalindmillercakes.com
www.gccouture.co.uk

Calligraphy
www.paulantonioscribe.com
www.calligraphycompany.com

Candles
www.shearer-candles.com

Caterers
www.admirable-crichton.co.uk
www.bywordofmouth.co.uk
www.mosimann.com
www.mustardcatering.com
www.rhubarb.net
www.lastsupperltd.co.uk
www.eclare.com
www.alisonprice.co.uk
www.absolutetaste.com
www.tonypage.com
www.carolesobell.com
www.foodamour.co.uk
www.wendymilbankltd.com

Dance Classes
www.firstdanceuk.co.uk
www.staroftheparty.com

Destination Weddings
www.farandfaraway.com
www.destinations.davidbeahm.com
www.destinationweddings.com

Event Production
www.starlightdesign.co.uk
www.dreamevents.com
www.banana-split.com
www.wiseproductions.co.uk
www.eventconcept.co.uk

Floral Designers
www.paulapryke.com
www.johncarterflowers.com
www.rvhfloraldesign.com
www.simonlycett.co.uk
www.shaneconnolly.com
www.tiger-rose.co.uk
www.michael-pooley-flowers.co.uk
www.maryjanevaughan.co.uk
www.neillstrain.com
www.paulthomasflowers.co.uk
www.veeverscarter.co.uk

Gift List
www.davidmellordesign.com
www.weddingshop.com
www.liberty.co.uk
www.prezola.com
www.notonthehighstreet.com
www.etsy.com

Address Book

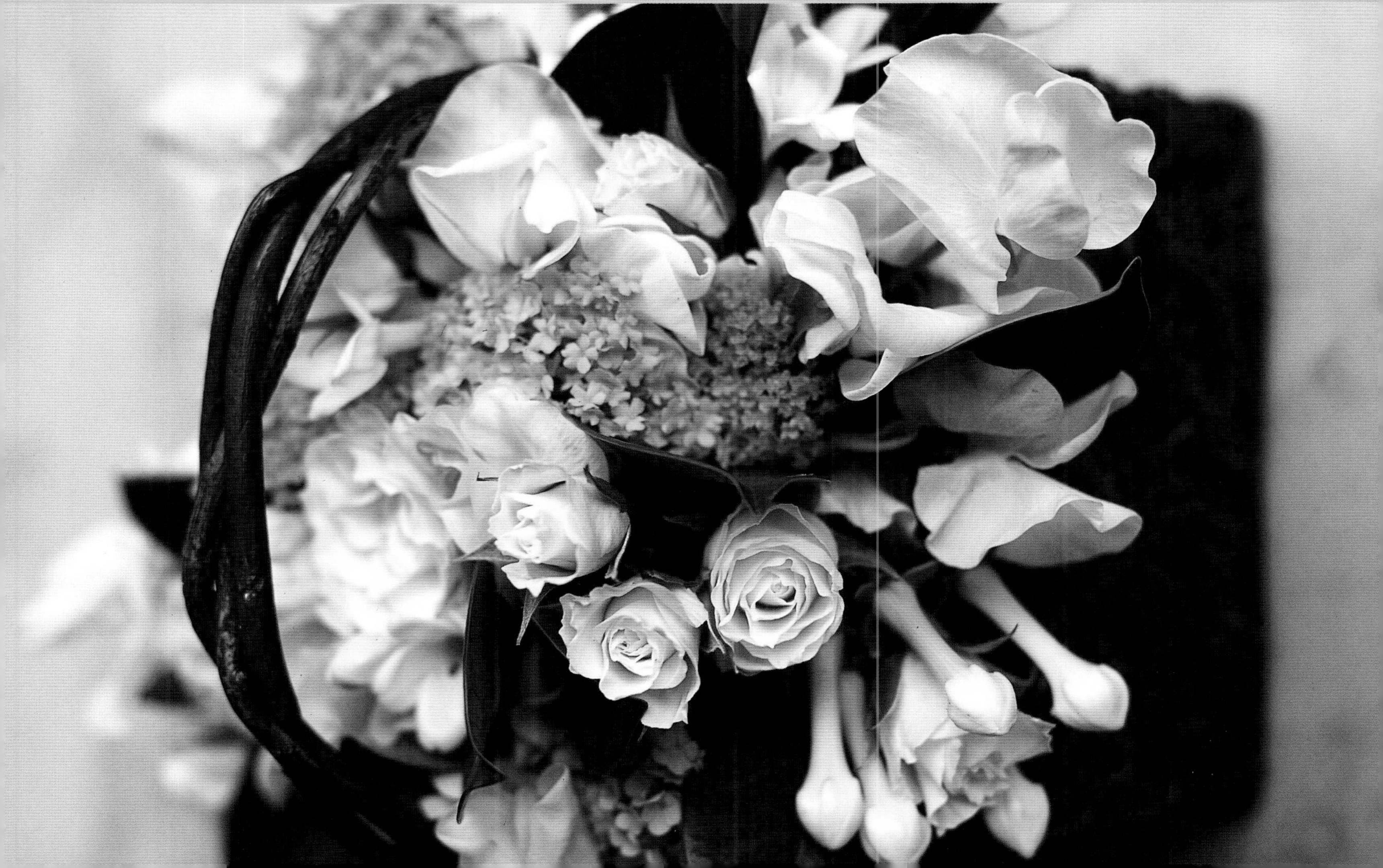

Gloves

www.dents.co.uk
www.sermonetagloves.com

Grooms

www.favourbrook.com
www.ozwaldboateng.co.uk
www.alexandermcqueen.com
www.buckleighoflondon.com

Hair and Make-up

www.vanclarke.com
www.hepburncollection.com
www.weddingmakeupandhair.com
www.danielhersheson.com
www.thestateofgrace,com
www.mariamjensen.com
www.karenbeadle.com
www.macs-salon.co.uk

Hats

www.edwinaibbotson.co.uk
www.philipsomerville.com
www.philiptreacy.co.uk
www.stephenjonesmillinery.com
www.racheltrevormorgan.com
www.fortnumandmason.com
www.straightupstyle.com

Insurance

www.robinsrow.com
www.johnlewis.com

Marquee Hire

www.rajtentclub.com
www.peppersmarquees.co.uk
www.fewsmarquees.co.uk
www.hadleymarquees.com
www.thepearltentcompany.com

Music

www.sternbergclarke.co.uk
www.mattmaurice.co.uk
www.urbansoulorchestra.co.uk
www.katyaherman.com

Photography

www.contre-jour.co.uk
www.damianbailey.com
www.photographybycatherine.co.uk
www.sarahvivienne.co.uk
www.kevinmullinsphotography.co.uk
www.lucytanner.com
www.pippamackenzie.com

www.mariannetaylorphotography.co.uk
www.jasminephotography.co.uk
www.fotonovo.com
www.steveshipmanphotography.com/
www.wildweddings.co.uk

Shoes

www.emmahope.com
www.frenchsole.com
www.prettyballerinas.com
www.jimmychoo.com
www.upperstreet.com
www.beatrixong.com
www.charlotteolympia.com

Spas

www.thedorchester.com
www.mandarinoriental.com
www.urbanretreat.co.uk
www.babingtonhouse.co.uk
www.thegrove.co.uk

Stationery

www.smythson.com
www.wrenpress.com
www.cutture.com
www.letterpress.co.uk
www.lovelyfavours.co.uk
www.ruthkayedesign.com

Tansport

www.karmakabs.com

Venues

www.highclerecastle.co.uk
www.sudeleycastle.co.uk
www.belvoircastle.com
www.thedorchester.com
www.fairmont.com
www.langhamhotels.co.uk
www.mosimann.com
www.claridges.co.uk
www.gaynespark.co.uk
www.syonpark.co.uk
www.kew.org
www.blenheimpalace.com
Kensington Palace Orangery www.hrp.org.uk
Holland Park Orangery www.rbkc.gov.uk
Victoria & Albert Museum www.vam.ac.uk
www.clivedenhouse.co.uk
www.aynhoepark.co.uk
www.manoir.com
www.coworthpark.com
www.the-vineyard.co.uk

www.noburestaurants.com
www.castleashbyweddings.co.uk
www.marcorestaurant.org

Videography
www.fxfilms.co.uk
www.thedreamcatchers.co.uk
www.filmatography.com

Wedding Blogs
www.lovemydress.net
www.bridesupnorth.co.uk
www.english-wedding.com
www.rockmywedding.co.uk
www.theweddinggirl.co.uk
www.weddinggowntown.com
www.thechiefbridesmaid.co.uk
www.greenunion.co.uk
www.beforethebigday.co.uk
www.ethicalweddings.com
www.london-bride.com

www.flowerona.com
www.omgimgettingmarried.com
www.rocknrollbride.com
www.segeriusbruceblog.com

Wedding Planners
www.siobhancraven-robins.co.uk
www.snapdragonparties.com
www.niemierko.com
www.sarahhaywood.com
www.ternevents.com
www.lillingston.co.uk
www.brideandglory.co.uk
www.amandasherlock.co.uk
www.lindacooperweddings.com
www.lestergatherings.com
www.collection26.com
www.bybrucerussell.com
www.tigerlilyweddings.co.uk
www.endless-love.co.uk
www.ukawp.com

THIS PAGE Roses, *Zinnia* 'Envy', hydrangea, *Viburnum opulus* berries and cotinus.
PREVIOUS PAGE A basket of white rosebuds, sweet peas and stephanotis.

USA

Accessories
www.mercinewyork.com
www.jenniferbehr.com
www.kleinfeldbridal.com

Bridal Gowns
www.verawang.com
www.moniquelhuillier.com
www.oscardelarenta.com
www.pronovias.com
www.carolinaherrera.com
www.ariadress.com
www.christosbridal.com
www.rivini.com
www.annebarge.com
www.kennethpool.com
www.moderntrousseau.com
www.watters.com
www.dessy.com
www.amsale.com

Bridesmaids
www.twobirdsbridesmaid.com
www.lelarose.com

Calligraphy
www.primele.com
www.betsydunlap.com

Cakes
www.thebutterend.com
www.flowerandflour.com
www.lovestreetcakes.com
www.wendykromer.com
www.sylviaweinstock.com

Catering
www.24carrots.com
www.ocnyc.com
www.lauriearons.com
www.crucatering.com
www.wimberleycatering.com
www.petercallahan.com
www.calderclark.com
www.paulaleduc.com
www.whoanellycatering.com

Event and Floral Design
www.wildflowerdesigns.net
www.bowsandarrowsflowers.com
www.davidbeahm.com
www.botanicaflorist.com

www.collegeflowers.com
www.marksgarden.com
www.inwaterflowers.com
www.davidstarkdesign.com
www.winstonflowers.com
www.mindyrice.com
www.saltharbor.com
www.brillianteventplanning.com
www.matthewrobbinsdesign.com
www.loopflowers.com
www.seaportflowers.com
www.saipua.com
www.paintedtulipvt.com
www.poppiesandposies.com
www.maxgilldesign.com
www.bashplease.com

Entertainment and Production
www.encoreproductions.ws
www.your-bash.com

Gift List
www.katespade.com
www.williams-sonoma.com
www.bloomingdales.com
www.macys.com
www.waterford.com
www.verawang.com

Grooms
www.zegna.com

Inspiration
www.marthastewartweddings.com
www.lulupowers.com
www.bridalbar.com

Marquees
www.tentprofessionals.com
www.sperrytents.com

Mixologists
Talmage Lowe www.pharmaciela.com
Tony Abou-Ganim www.themodernmixologist.com

Photography
www.featherlove.com
www.christianothstudio.com
www.brookeschwabphotography.com
www.sylviegilphotography.com

Rentals
www.classicpartyrentals.com
www.partyrentalltd.com
www.luxeeventrentals.com
www.savannahspecialevents.com

Rings Worldwide
www.debeers.com
www.cartier.com

Stationery
www.bellafigura.com
www.blackbirdletterpress.com
www.ladyfingersletterpress.com
www.mygatsby.com
www.maemaepaperie.com
www.papercupdesign.com
www.stripeandfield.com
www.weddingpaperdivas.com
www.minted.com
www.invitationsbydawn.com

Venues
www.sanysidroranch.com
www.thecarnerosinn.com
www.bluehillfarm.com
www.redcorralranch.com
www.winecountry.com

Videographer
www.sixminutestories.com

Wedding Blogs
www.stylemepretty.com
www.thebridesguide.marthastewartweddings.com
www.100layercake.com
www.bridalbuds.com
www.designsponge.com
www.greenweddingshoes.com
www.weddingchicks.com
www.diybride.com
www.flirtyfleurs.com

Wedding Planners
www.loveandsplendor.com
www.thebridalbar.com
www.alexandrak.com
www.lauriearons.com
www.carsonsweddings.com
www.bashplease.com

Australia

Bridal Gowns
www.annacampbell.com.au
www.wattersbridal.com.au

Bridesmaids
www.tutudumonde.com

Caterers
www.artisticfood.com.au
www.flavourscatering.com.au
www.bluesorrento.com.au

Floral Designers
www.flowersanctuary.com.au
www.mossnstone.com.au
www.blossomandtwine.com.au
www.susanavery.com
www.budflowers.com
www.pollonflowers.com.au
www.artstems.com.au
www.flowersvasette.com.au
www.flowertemple.com

Gift List
www.girlfridayweddings.com
www.theweddingnest.com.au
www.donnahay.com.au/giftregistry

Inspiration
www.donnahay.com.au
www.hitchedmag.com.au

Marquees
www.overtop.com.au

Photography
www.reedphotography.com.au

Wedding Blogs
www.polkadotbride.com
www.thestyleco.com.au

Wedding Planners
www.wpaa.net.au
www.alavishaffair.com

Acknowledgements

Grateful thanks to all our contributors for their words of wisdom:

Tony Abou-Garmin
Author and Mixologist
www.themodernmixologist.com

Damian Bailey
Wedding Photographer, Blogger and Founder of
The Wedding Industry Awards
www.damianbailey.com
www.the-wedding-industry-awards.co.uk

Siobhan Craven-Robbins
Wedding Coordinator
www.siobhancraven.com

Richard Cubbin
Executive Chef and Director of Alison Price
Catering
www.alisonprice.co.uk

Julia Dowling
Event Planning and Wedding Coordinator
MD of Snapdragon Parties
www.snapdragonparties.com

Pauline Milbank
Caterer and Event Planner
www.foodamour.co.uk

Wendy Milbank
Caterer and Event Planner
www.wendymilbankltd.com

Bruce Oldfield OBE
Bridal Couturier
www.bruceoldfield.com

Roger Pizey
Author and Executive Chef of Marco Restaurant
www.marcorestaurant.org

Mich Turner MBE
Author and Director of Little Venice Cake
Company
www.lvcc.co.uk

Photography Credits

Pages 1, 4, bottom right 17, 20, top right 21, 27, 35, 40, 41, 53, 54, 94, top right 117, 119, top & bottom left 130, 136, 137, 144, 147 all photography is by Sian Irvine.

Pages 5, 9, top right 17, 23, 31, 32, 33, 34, 37, 68, 69, 75, 76, 77, 79, 82, 84, 85, 87, 89, 92, 93, 98, 99, 100, 101, inset 111, 115, top left 117, bottom right 117, 118, 128, top right and bottom left 129, 133, 138, 139, 145 all photography is by Polly Wreford.

Pages 7, 14, 15, 16, top left 17, 18, 19, 24, 25, 29, 36, 49, 50, 58, 59, 60, 61, 62, 63, 64, 66, 67, 71, 72, 73, 74, 81, 86, 90, 91, 141, 157 all photography is by Sarah Cuttle.

Pages 2, 3, 10, 11, 13, bottom left 17, bottom 21, 26, 30, 39, 42, 43, 45, 46, 48, 50, 52, 55, 56, 78, 104, 105, 106, 108, 109, 110, top 111, 113, 116, bottom left 117, 120, 121, 122, 123, 124, 125, 127, bottom right 129, top & bottom right 130, 134, 135, 140, 142, 148, 149, 155 all photography is by Chris Tubbs.

Pages 22, 102, top left 129, 132 all photography is by Rachel Whiting.

First published in 2013 by
Jacqui Small LLP
An imprint of Aurum Press
74–77 White Lion Street
London N1 9PF

Publisher: Jacqui Small
Managing Editor: Lydia Halliday
Designer: Maggie Town
Editor: Sian Parkhouse
Production: Maeve Healy

ISBN: 978 1 909342 37 8
A catalogue record for this book
is available from the British Library.

2015 2014 2013
10 9 8 7 6 5 4 3 2 1

Printed in China